Pra

Sales & Mark...

Sales and marketing alignment is essential in today's digital world. Companies and business leaders must find ways to generate synergies from their teams and avoid conflict. Tom and Karl have excellent advice in this book and have developed a winning road map to bring the alignment necessary to unlock sales growth.
—Donald Myers, Vistage Master Chair

Sales and marketing are two different and equally critical functions. The rapid and rampant changes brought on by technology, shifting demographics and processes make each more complex. This well-researched work focuses on helping you align them, an increasingly critical activity for organizations that intend to grow in the post-pandemic era. Keep a notepad handy. Your customers will thank you.
—Chuck Reaves, CSP, CPAE, CSO, Author of *The Nanosecond Salesperson— Like the One-minute Salesperson Only Faster*

Symbiotic convergence of marketing, sales and technology is what will define market leaders of this century, and it starts not with tools and tricks but with deep alignment of multidisciplinary functions. Karl and Thomas's book shows a practical way of approaching this problem.
—Alex Natskovich, CEO, MEV

This book is a must-read for anyone starting or ramping up a company. I am going to give a copy to every cohort that goes through the Softeq Venture Studio.
—Bret Siarkowski, Founder, Softeq Venture Fund & Studio

This is THE go-to manual for aligning sales and marketing teams.
—**John Arnott,** CEO, ContentFirst.Marketing

At long last, we have the definitive, practical, comprehensive yet detailed road map to the holy grail of sales and marketing integration. The authors compellingly explain why this integration is necessary and provide clear methods, processes and action steps for creating a lasting solution that aligns all stakeholders, team members and customers. This will be a must-read book for all CEOs in my Vistage groups.
—**Karen Meenan,** Vistage Chair

How many times have you wanted to chain your sales and marketing teams together...and drop them into the ocean? *Sales & Marketing Alignment* explains through compelling stories and practical step-by-step instructions how to eliminate the silos that pull sales and marketing away from one another. As if that wasn't valuable enough, the authors explain in detail how an aligned organization actually works! This book should be on the corner of every SMB executive's desk.
—**Tom Stimson,** President, Stimson Group LLC

Marketing is expensive: click costs, management and SEO can be a waste of time and money when sales and marketing aren't working together as a well-oiled machine. Karl and Thomas have created an excellent guidebook for marketing and sales teams to work better together. This book provides a missing piece of the puzzle and is an excellent strategic blueprint for any digital marketing campaign.
—**Jim Kreinbrink,** President, Hyper Dog Media

This book is what every business needs to read. I constantly see the separation of sales and marketing departments, and the accusations that get flung onto each. The authors say it best with this statement:

Foster an attitude of gratitude between teams! Encourage the sales team to share wins and thank marketing for their work to qualify leads and share data, and marketing to thank sales for sharing firsthand experiences with leads and customers.

This is how sales and marketing should work.

—Steven Devries, Principal, Sayvee.com

One of the greatest blockers of company growth that I've seen is sales and marketing teams that are siloed, communicating different messaging and pointing fingers at each other at every point of failure. In order for businesses to reach their full potential, sales and marketing have to work together like the left and right hands of a revenue-generating engine. The book *Sales & Marketing Alignment* provides clear and simple guidance, tools and action items to do just that. It outlines precisely how to ensure the right people use the right processes in developing, implementing and optimizing the right strategies that result in sales growth from the right market. This has a significantly positive impact on culture and morale in the organization as well as valuation. Tom and Karl are both teachers at heart, and any reader will benefit tenfold from implementing their methods.

—Leila Blauner, Founder and Team Growth Strategist, Scalability Solutions

I really valued reading *Sales & Marketing Alignment*. As the founder and president of my company, [I found] the topics hit home and resonated with where we have been and where we want to go. As the leader of the company, I now have a blueprint to bring my sales and marketing teammates together to be more aligned and effective. Thank you!

—Garry Hale, President and Founder, AVentPro

Breaking down dysfunctional and adversarial relationships between sales and marketing is fundamental to success in today's business environment. This book breaks down simple, practical advice on how to bridge gaps between teams rather than fence them to your own detriment. The lesson that this book teaches is one that every business leader needs to learn, and quickly.

—Erik Wolf, Author, Unified Marketing System

Sales & Marketing Alignment reveals Karl Becker and Tom Young's mastery of their craft. It reveals strategic and tactical steps to take on how to improve a sales and marketing organization, and where it really excels is in its ability to clearly communicate how to collaborate with others, to break down silos and bring organizations closer together.

—Theo Tehrani, Business Development and Revenue Consultant, Entrepreneur, Investor

Whether you're new to business or a veteran with decades of experience, this book will give you a distinct advantage. Creating successful sales and marketing teams can be a complex puzzle. Tom and Karl help you get into the minds of each of the players, including leadership, sales, marketing and the customer, and then provide action items for each step of the way. Digital marketing is included, which I found super helpful. I highly recommend each member of your team get a copy of this book!

—Sylvia Theisen, Executive and Life Coach, Prime Time Coaching

This book is spot on. Marketing and sales have changed significantly, and far too many leaders are still spinning their wheels in silos. Karl and Tom do a great job of defining the purpose and function of marketing vs. sales, and how to bring the two together for massive success. Bonus—this isn't a book based on theory…it's super practical with opportunities to implement immediately!

—Ali Schwanke, Founder of Simple Strat, Host of HubSpot Hacks

CEOs, if you haven't noticed that the keys to "selling and marketing" success have dramatically changed in the last few years, it will not turn out well for you. Moreover, sales and marketing cannot be viewed or managed as silos. Both functions can't *not* have your full attention as the CEO of your company. As a long time CEO coach and an attentive student of how marketing and selling has truly changed from the days when I was a CEO, I told Tom and Karl that the world needed a book like theirs. It appropriately focuses on the organizational alignment of these two functions and provides an excellent set of tools for CEOs to get involved themselves and drive the growth of their company.

—Lonnie Martin, Vistage Chair

SALES & MARKETING ALIGNMENT

SALES & MARKETING ALIGNMENT

Break Down Silos, Get Unstuck and Succeed as a Team

Karl Becker & Thomas Young

First Printing 2022

ISBN 979-8-218-01409-4

Improving Sales Performance
Improvingsalesperformance.com

Intuitive Websites
Intuitivewebsites.com

Contents

Introduction:
It's Time for a Sales and Marketing Transformation

Prepare to see better sales and marketing results from a unified team.

Welcome to your sales and marketing alignment journey. We are grateful you chose to improve your sales and marketing results by reading our book! You are starting on a path to less risk and less uncertainty for your business and stronger teamwork between your sales and marketing departments, leading to business growth and marketing success.

The main objective of *Sales & Marketing Alignment: Break Down Silos, Get Unstuck and Succeed as a Team* **is to show business professionals, particularly those in leadership, how to think differently about the tasks and roles of sales and marketing teams in the age of digital marketing and selling.** This new way of thinking can be used to integrate your sales and marketing functions, leading to more impressive results.

The internet has both provided companies a tremendous marketing channel to reach new customers and made reaching those new customers more competitive than ever. Millions of websites, videos, ads and digital posts compete for our attention, and many salespeople struggle to find interested and qualified prospects.

Following the principles in this book will help you market better, sell more effectively and gain a competitive advantage in today's noisy business environment. What you will learn comes from our real-life experiences with hundreds of companies in a variety of industries. We have consulted and trained thousands of sales and marketing professionals to perform at higher levels. You are getting key insights that work in the real world of sales and marketing. This book shows you how to coordinate those efforts to maintain and grow sales.

We hope you use *Sales & Marketing Alignment* as a stepping-stone to highly effective sales and marketing strategies and tactics, driving business growth for years to come. Let's get started!

Part One:

Effective Sales and Marketing Alignment Is Strategic

Chapter 1:
The Power of Strategic Alignment in Sales and Marketing

Discover the missing piece holding back many sales and marketing teams from reaching their goals.

This chapter previews the concepts and principles we cover in this book to help you get your sales and marketing teams aligned, integrated and achieving results.

Imagine you're conducting an orchestra. Your goal is to lead the musicians in performing a beautiful piece of music that will keep your entire audience enraptured, ending with a roaring round of applause. You have all the elements in place to make this happen: experienced musicians, a moving score and a skilled conductor with all the passion in the world.

Now imagine that when everyone starts playing, you're hit with ear-splitting noise. You have all the individual elements you need to wow your audience, so why aren't you getting the results you want?

It's aggravating to not know what's going wrong, whether you are a conductor aiming for a pitch-perfect symphony or a business leader in pursuit of positive sales results. Unfortunately, we see many real-world business owners struggling with discord and poor performance with their sales and marketing efforts, unsure what they need to fix.

Closing sales to generate business and keep a company running is essential. Business leaders are also responsible for managing endless moving parts, much like a conductor who has multiple musicians to guide. With so much going on, it can be difficult to put a finger on what's causing sales to suffer. There could be a team of excellent players—salespeople with amazing close rates; marketers who write clever, engaging copy; designers who build gorgeous websites—but without a well-planned sales and marketing strategy, the result is efforts thwarted from within and miscalculations. Without first coming together to practice before a concert, an orchestra only creates a bunch of noise.

If you're reading this book, you are most likely a business leader or enthusiastic sales or marketing professional who is open to change and improvement. You care about your team and want to explore any ideas that will improve revenue and the performance of your sales and marketing teams. However, if you don't have the proper perspective when it comes to valuing sales and marketing alignment, you may not be providing the kind of leadership that will help your sales organization succeed.

Every member of an orchestra needs to start the same song on the same page at the same time, then look to the conductor to stay in time and create something that wows the crowd. Your sales and marketing organization needs to come together and act as one in the same way. To bring sales and marketing into alignment and achieve the harmony of healthy revenue, you must lead that change.

Helping Find Your Path Forward

If you are at a loss to explain why your sales aren't succeeding and growing in the way you want, you're not alone. When we reflected upon the hundreds of small- to medium-size business (SMB) client engagements we've undertaken in the past decade, we came to a startling realization. Not even one of them had an intentionally designed sales and marketing organization before we came into the picture.

To be sure, some of them had created solid websites, marketing campaigns, CRM installations and sales training. However, the lead capture-and-nurture process was always problematic, and there were multiple places where leads would fall through the cracks.

The principles in this book provide you with the know-how you need to get your people in sync and your processes set, and they show you how to lead in a way that creates beautiful results. In our experience, these methods have helped numerous organizations get back in alignment and start increasing their sales and revenue.

Meet Your Guides

We, Karl Becker and Thomas Young, bring a combined fifty years of experience in sales and marketing, living and breathing it through consulting and building businesses of our own. We have developed sales and marketing systems and processes, always evolving with the times, always pivoting whenever and wherever necessary and never resting on our laurels.

Karl ran digital agencies before transitioning to sales leadership as a consultant, trainer and author. His book *Set Up to Win* was published in spring of 2021 and offers three frameworks to build a sales organization that is stable and able to grow.

Tom spent ten years managing corporate sales teams and then worked as a sales consultant and trainer. He wrote *Intuitive Selling* in 2000, which offers a holistic and innovative approach to getting sales results. In 2004, Tom launched the digital marketing firm Intuitive Websites, which has served hundreds of clients. In 2014, Tom published *Winning the Website War*, which provides a four-step process for getting better results from a business's website marketing efforts.

The two of us met at a roundtable of a peer mentoring organization for CEOs, business owners and executives of SMBs called Vistage International. As we began our collaboration on the integration of sales and marketing teams, we quickly discovered that we share the same sales and marketing DNA. We both like to build and test processes, exchange knowledge and diagnose and solve business problems that many organizations would consider terminal errors. To that end, we have presented to thousands of business leaders throughout North America and helped nearly a thousand clients raise their games.

Sales teams can't thrive without the kind of work Karl and his organization does. Marketing teams can't thrive without the kind of work Tom and his team do. We've put every one of our theories to the test, evolving our businesses with the times. The ideas shared in this book are tried, applied and tested, and we're confident they'll help you get unstuck.

We know that companies today are dealing with talent shortages, escalating salaries, complex and expensive technologies, competitors' private equity financing and more. There is an increased awareness that teamwork, leadership and technology are all important. However, while awareness is elevated, the path forward isn't always clear.

What to Expect from This Book

Our intention is to help you understand how sales and marketing alignment is built around strategy, processes and people. We focus on what you need to integrate sales and marketing effectively so that you can create higher-performing teams, foster greater accountability and achieve your revenue goals in today's competitive marketplace.

Your Strategies

If you're like other leaders we've worked with, you've probably been focusing on one solution to solve your sales and revenue problems: more leads. In our experience, that approach usually doesn't end up where people wish it would.

Achieving your sales goals goes way beyond getting leads. Here, we show you how to think strategically and how an integrated sales and marketing approach can change the game for your organization. We also talk about how to incorporate intentional digital marketing into your overall strategy and why it's vital you do so.

Your Processes

You may have heard of sales funnels, but can you tell us what happens to your leads once they're in there? Can you tell us who is responsible for each stage of the sales funnel and how a lead gets passed from one stage to the next? We review the concept of the sales funnel and show you how to integrate sales and marketing into it, passing leads from stage to stage and through every step in the buyer's journey. We also show you how to make sure leads don't get stuck in the funnel in that mysterious middle section between sales and marketing. By the time you're done, everyone in your organization should know their role in turning a lead into a customer.

Your People

Often, sales and marketing are siloed, meaning they're off doing their own things without coordinating and collaborating on strategy and processes. In these cases, when companies don't hit their sales goals, sales says marketing gave them bad leads who were not prepared to buy. Marketing complains the sales team dropped the ball and only thinks about their commissions instead of building relationships.

This siloed approach doesn't work. Everyone must play a role in your company's sales and marketing success. Our goal is to give the people in your company the awareness and knowledge to maximize their sales and marketing efforts through teamwork and communication. We help you build sales and marketing teams who share perspectives and goals and are ready to work together on strategies and tactics.

Get Honest About Your Leadership

By picking up this book, you've shown that you know something needs to change in sales and marketing to create revenue growth. You and other leadership at your company are responsible for guiding your sales and marketing team to play in harmony, just like a conductor guides musicians in an orchestra. *Sales & Marketing Alignment* asks you to consider your attitudes and actions toward your sales and marketing departments to determine whether you are nurturing sales or killing them.

By the end of this book, you will be able to do the following:

- Identify key strategies to maximize sales and marketing performance.

- Structure sales and marketing funnels to better manage leads and maximize revenue.

- Eliminate the barriers between your sales and marketing teams to implement the strategies and tactics you've developed without leads becoming stuck in those funnels.

There is no quick fix to sales and marketing growth, so if you're looking for a silver bullet, you won't find it here. However, if you're willing to put the work in, you will get clarity on how to develop strategies, processes and people in ways that will propel you to your goals.

Chapter 2:
If You Build It, They May Ignore You

"Putting something out there" isn't good enough to attract leads and turn them into customers.

This chapter demonstrates why strategic intent is necessary to help your sales and marketing strategies stand out in an increasingly competitive business environment.

With increased competition and greater digital savvy among businesses and potential customers, many companies struggle to rise above the noise and be heard. Having a great product or service is not enough. Using common sales and marketing strategies may not be either. This can leave business owners wondering where they have gone wrong. In the worst case, it can put them out of business.

Adapt or Fall Behind

Robert is CEO of Team Discovery, a niche educational software company he founded some twenty years ago. (*Note: We have chosen to use pseudonyms for companies and people mentioned in this book.*) When he started out, he had no trouble signing customers; in fact, they were coming in droves to him. However, in recent years, numerous direct competitors have started to chip away at Team Discovery's revenue to the tune of a 5–10 percent decline for each of the past five years.

In response, Robert put lots of pressure on the company's sales director and chief marketing officer (CMO) to turn things around, which in turn put everybody on edge. A steady flow of inquiries came in each week, but sales were flat.

The CMO perceived most marketing strategies as guessing games and many digital marketing tactics as wastes of time. So, the marketing team threw a new figurative coat of paint on the website, updated the company brochure, posted to Facebook a few times a year, updated the proposal boilerplate and spent a few thousand dollars a month on Google Ads. They also continued switching digital marketing firms every six months, which meant a clear strategy never took hold, with no chance to fix what was not working.

Meanwhile, the sales team relied on current customers, industry relationships and strong referral networks to land new business. Each day, the sales director and her team willed the phone to ring and took orders from the few leads who were ready to buy, struggling with leads who were not already sold on their software and blaming the CMO for sending "unqualified leads."

Things got so bad the sales director and CMO decided to jump ship, leaving Robert as the de facto head of both the sales and marketing departments.

"Help me understand what's going on," Robert said to them during their exit interviews.

"We need better leads from marketing," the sales director said.

"We are getting sales leads, but the competition is too strong," the CMO said.

Robert knows neither of them were correct. Their competitors' products are more expensive and less user-friendly, with fewer features, lots of bugs and a lack of sufficient customer support. Robert doesn't understand how or why they were so successful at impacting Team Discovery's business.

Based on our experience with clients who have had similar problems, we do understand. Other businesses are outselling Team Discovery because they have done the following:

- Built integrated, intentional sales and marketing engines aligned with how businesses grow in today's digital spaces

- Hired and trained a focused marketing team and a large team of sales reps prepared to adopt forward-thinking lead-nurture processes

- Cultivated their leads at every stage, systematizing the steps involved in closing them

Robert and his team did not adapt to the ways business was changing and were therefore falling behind. Much of this issue could be improved by changing the way sales and marketing were run. Here are a few lessons we've learned over the years that could help Robert get his business back on track.

Lesson One: Sales and Marketing Teams Must Adapt

Change is hard for sales and marketing teams. Many folks want to hang on to what worked in the past, and they struggle to navigate an evolving sales and marketing landscape. Marketing recognizes the company's social following is meager, their website visits are low and their Google Ads aren't hitting the mark, but building a base of raving fans isn't exactly their forte.

At the same time, sales are getting leads who want to learn more but aren't ready to sign on the dotted line. Instead of nurturing those leads, they say, "Call me when you're ready to buy." That's not selling; that's just taking down orders.

Companies often wait as long as possible to acknowledge that they don't know what to do. Sometimes, they expand problematic sales systems, which makes them more inefficient. They watch as some of their competitors thrive and wonder why they can't keep up.

Stress and tension grow. They hope the problem will magically be fixed, and when it's not, they start to panic.

Marketing teams can no longer depend on pretty websites and periodic social posts and wait for their next tactical assignment. Salespeople can no longer live and die by the ringing phone. The sales and marketing of yesteryear simply cannot compete in today's hyper-strategic, systematized digital age.

Lesson Two: Sales and Marketing Are Experiencing Massive Disruption

Two massive changes are happening in sales and marketing, both of which are accelerated by leaps in digital technology. These offer the keys to how your business must adapt to survive.

Buyers Will Research You Before You Ever Speak with Them

With dozens, hundreds or even thousands of online sources on most any topic, buyers have an embarrassment of informational riches at their disposal. By following you on social media and reading articles, forums and reviews, they learn all about you before making person-to-person contact.

In addition to the sheer amount of information, another challenge is that the audience's attention has been commoditized. Spam, click bait, scammers, automatic opt-ins and data breaches have eroded trust.

Yes, there is an opportunity here since it's easier for your target audience to discover you. But buyers today are shrewd, which makes them harder to convert. They want to find you and initiate contact rather than being found and pursued by you. Therefore, your team needs to know how to make yourselves more attractive to them and differentiate yourselves both from scammers and from legitimate competitors.

Competition Has Intensified, and Adding Value Is Mandatory

Many companies are rising above this incredible amount of distraction and noise in order to be found, build trust and win customers. Companies who accept the new reality are using technology to their advantage by adopting automation and strategic sales and marketing processes. They are communicating real benefits directly with leads and using value-adding online resources to attract them. Their sales teams are ready to meet customers where they are on their own journeys toward solving the challenges their offers might address.

You must offer value to your leads from the beginning and throughout their journey from new prospect to paying customer. If you don't, you will be drowned out by companies who are giving more and guiding leads through their well-designed sales funnels.

That means you need to create strategic processes too, and that can only happen if your sales and marketing systems work together.

Lesson Three: Sales and Marketing Need Each Other (And Effective Leadership)

You saw what happened to Team Discovery—their marketing department conducted haphazard campaigns (if you could even call them that), and sales didn't nurture leads through a journey to turn them into customers. Their CEO put pressure on them without bringing them together to create a strategic vision based on adapting to the changes around them. When things went wrong, everyone blamed one another instead of pulling together.

To keep from falling into the blame game as leads fall through the cracks, sales and marketing must coordinate their efforts and work together to drive business growth. Leaders at every level are responsible for uniting them. Sales and marketing must seamlessly guide the prospect from their inquiry to purchase by providing the following:

Marketing Team	Sales Team
Clear info	Answers to questions
Value	Replies to concerns
Benefits	Instructions for getting started
Next steps for working with sales	

Sales and marketing teams must align their efforts and create an honest-to-goodness plan that doesn't rely on their lead base to do all the heavy lifting. They need to identify and go after new markets and, perhaps most importantly, stop inadvertently ignoring or entirely abandoning the leads and customers already in the pipeline.

To foster real change, sales and marketing teams need to see the bigger picture. One cannot function without the other.

Do Your Sales and Marketing Teams Work Together?

Aligning and integrating the efforts of sales and marketing teams are non-negotiables if you want to improve organizational efficiency and increase revenue. Companies that integrate sales and marketing into a cohesive team will gain a substantial advantage against the competition. Here are three questions to ask yourself as you evaluate how your sales and marketing team can be more successful:

1. Do we have an integrated sales and marketing funnel?

2. Do we know who owns each stage of the sales and marketing funnel?

3. Does our team have resources to move prospects from stage to stage in the funnel?

If you can't answer yes to all these questions, the competition will drown you. If you don't have a plan in place, no amount of marketing emails or sales calls will keep you above water.

It's the sales and marketing teams' jobs to optimize each step toward making a purchase—aka the buyer's journey—for every type of customer. That can't happen unless everyone in the organization commits to playing on the same team to serve its best interests and the best interests of the company.

We teach you the value of an integrated sales and marketing funnel and how it can become a reliable and effective system to progress from early prospect generation to the point of purchase. This integration means that each person in sales and marketing must know what stage of that funnel is their responsibility and how to pass the ball to the next team member to score that final goal: a sale.

Once everyone knows their role in the funnel and you have gone through the process of developing resources and action plans for addressing each category of customer you serve, you will start to score more and more goals. Adapting all the while, you will find those points add up to big wins.

Are you ready to do the hard work to unite your team, design your strategy and implement the processes you need to make your company thrive in a changing business landscape? Are you ready to build something that helps you stand out among your competitors, something that prospective customers will notice rather than ignore? The following chapter tells you the three guiding concepts to integrating your sales and marketing teams and achieving your business goals.

Chapter 3:
The Three Pillars of Success: Strategy, Processes and People

These three areas are key to building a highly productive sales and marketing machine.

This chapter shares what it takes to build effective strategies, how processes make those strategies possible to execute and who makes all the magic happen.

We've referenced three areas that absolutely must work together to drive sales and revenue growth: strategy, processes and people. Let's clarify the definition of each of them.

For the purposes of this book, *strategy* is the overarching game plan setting the direction in which you want to head. *Processes*, which include the tactics you use or steps you take, are the systems used to implement your strategy. *People* are not just warm bodies but the right team members for the jobs at hand.

You can have great processes and people, but you'll have trouble achieving ambitious sales goals without an overarching strategy. You can have a great strategy and great processes, but if you have the wrong people in sales, marketing and key leadership positions, you're sure to flounder. You can have a great strategy and great people, but without established, evolving processes to follow, those people will have to work harder, with no space to work smarter, to reach the same results.

Everything Starts with Strategy

Another way to define *strategy* is "taking the right actions to reach a goal." It can also be seen as an understanding of your mission and goals and the ability to select the right path to get there. Sales and marketing strategies make or break everything we talk about in this book as they set direction for processes and tactics. Strategy is a plan put into action. It identifies the right things to do and the right steps to take to achieve your business goals.

Many organizations' idea of strategy is to keep busy. This involves sales and marketing teams doing things, sometimes a lot of random things. They create more social media posts, run more ads, launch new discounts and submit more boilerplate proposals. They make sales call after sales call.

We call this the "people doing things" model of sales and marketing— the strategy is "winging it." It relies on a few rainmakers to carry the major burden of driving sales and does little to maximize the team's potential.

Then there's strategy by accident, where leaders fall into tactics they inherited from someone else. This may not work as well as it did back when the plan was first implemented, but the newly minted sales director was told in no uncertain terms to make profits without making waves. She is excited to have landed the job, so rocking the boat is the last thing on her mind. However, she's at a loss as to how to close more deals using a dated strategy tailor-made for a different day and time.

Then we have a company whose owner saved money by building his own poorly designed website, managing his own social media pages and handling sales and marketing on his own. Eventually he hires a receptionist, who becomes the de facto marketing manager. "Why did our most recent Facebook post get only one like?" he asks her one morning. She shrugs and reminds him to call several prospects who reached out over the past week. "I've got fires to put out," he says. "I'll get to it when I can." We might call that the "no strategy at all" model.

All of these sales and marketing efforts are inefficient at best because they lack thought and intention, planning and design and concrete, scalable action. They lack strategy, process and the right people for the job.

A strategy works best as a longer-term play built upon your understanding of your clients' problems, wants and needs. **To build a goal-oriented strategy, you first need to know what's important to you—your values, mission, goals and target market, along with clearly identifiable ways in which you are stronger and more capable than your competition.** This solid foundation must come before all else if you truly want to move forward with effective sales and marketing work.

Strategy Requires Intentionality

Intentionality is about turning strategy into a concrete plan and managing according to the plan, which outlines the steps and priorities you need to take to achieve your intentional outcome. Strategy sets the direction for the sales and marketing tactics you develop. Companies rarely reach their sales goals by accident. Those that reach their sales goals almost always have an intentional strategy driving their growth.

Strategy Requires a Combination of Creativity and Logic

Strategy is more than just a thought or an idea—it's a way of envisioning your business. Great strategy is a blend of creativity and logic, measured in whatever parts yield the desired goal or outcome. It's a mindset you choose to follow that helps you achieve a designated future state. You must bring your team together to determine the creative tactics that work best combined with the logic to measure those results against your goals and mission.

Strategy Requires Action

Some people assume that when there is a good idea, everything else will just fall into place, and the idea will all but implement itself. Nothing could be further from the truth. Without action, ideas have no substance. Action means being serious about strategy and committed to seeing it through. It requires team alignment, mutual accountability and the ability to adapt and pivot. At all times, action should intentionally serve a specific, desired result.

Processes Make Strategy Possible

A clear strategy helps define the sales and marketing processes you build, and the specific tactics you use to implement these processes will drive results.

At the outset, process building can seem daunting. It takes time, money and staff resources. Some leaders don't want to go to the trouble and prefer to implement quick-fix processes on the fly. They duct tape tactics together rather than building a solid, systematized strategy.

Processes best serve your strategy when they are replicable, scalable and flexible enough to evolve when needed. While your processes will need to be adjusted as you acquire more information, the more organized you are, the more likely you are to experience wins.

Let's say you like to go to baseball games. Your dream is to catch a foul ball, but you've been to a hundred games over the years and never caught a single one. If you're one of twenty thousand fans in the stands and you're wondering why you've been left empty-handed, you probably haven't taken the steps necessary to increase your odds. You may not have tried tactics like avoiding the upper decks and instead sitting in the lower sections next to third or first base. You may not have tried showing up at more sparsely populated, middle-of-the week, midday games. You may not have considered making yourself more visible as a serious fan by wearing the home team's colors and bringing your kids with you, encouraging someone from the field to toss a ball your way (it's not the glory of catching a foul ball, but you'll take it!).

If you do try all these things, will you definitely catch a ball? Maybe not, but these tactics bring you closer to achieving your goal. Have you dramatically improved your odds? Absolutely. Catching a foul ball is tough, but without a strategy that's made of a series of small tactics, you have no chance whatsoever. Small, intentional steps can add up to a big win.

Processes Help You Map Strategies

We provide you with a helpful framework for taking your strategies and plotting out the processes used to close sales: the integrated sales and marketing funnel. This allows you to chart your strategy from taking action that catches leads' attention, through inviting them to learn more and engage with more marketing materials and then putting them in touch with salespeople who can close. Once you have a visual representation of these strategies, you can start breaking them down into processes and figuring out who will execute the tactics that comprise them. (Please note we sometimes use the shorthand *sales funnel* and sometimes *funnel* to refer to the integrated sales and marketing funnel.)

Processes Function Best through the Use of Automated Tools

There are many different tools available to carry your leads through the sales and marketing process and from one stage of the funnel to the next. Automating your processes will save you and your people time and expand the number of prospects you can reach. There are so many ways to clarify and automate your processes that it is beyond the scope of this book to list every possible one. Instead, we focus on how sales and marketing teams can create and organize these processes together.

Processes Help Your People Do Their Jobs

The members of your sales and marketing teams are responsible for adjusting, honing or pivoting your processes. A lot of confusion, buck passing and gaps in your processes can be avoided when your people are mapped to each process and stage of your funnel. Your effectiveness leaps even further when you arrange regular, helpful meetings to share knowledge between the sales and marketing teams.

Put the Right People in the Right Positions

Your people must share your values and mission, support your goals and understand and stand behind your strategy. They bring strategy to fruition by implementing winning processes and doing the actual work, or tactics.

Just like how the "winging it" model doesn't work for strategy, it doesn't work for people, either. Yet an absence of clearly defined roles is all too common in sales and marketing. So is sending in someone who is the wrong fit for a role. For example, an all-star closer who is told to take over managing the sales team may not understand why everyone is not a star closer and end up frustrating the rest of the team with his expectations. A sales wunderkind who is put in charge of the website may not have the necessary technical savvy, causing sales and revenues to drop as the website is repeatedly delayed. When talented people perform tasks wholly unsuited to them, it almost always ends in frustration and failure.

When you want to improve sales and marketing performance, cultivating employee interests and strengths is much more effective than trying to improve their weaknesses. Continue to build skills in areas where those individuals already excel and then stand back and watch them take your sales and marketing organization to new heights.

Defining Roles for Sales and Marketing

It comes down to this: marketing generates leads, and sales closes deals. Each specialty requires in-depth training, substantial on-the-job experience and a growing body of expertise regarding what works, what doesn't and why. These jobs are not interchangeable, and they are not positions that any warm body can fill.

If you want to grow and you don't have a strategy or a process or a trained sales and marketing team in place, your risk increases exponentially. It's also risky to have a solid strategy and the wrong process and people, as your strategy probably will never get off the ground.

Get the right people in the right seats performing the right tasks in accordance with proven processes. It takes a village (i.e., aligned sales and marketing teams) to stay on top of industry changes and competitive developments. You need a qualified, capable team to understand your strategy, embrace processes and take concrete action.

Getting Your People Involved in Your Alignment Efforts

Being strategic about who leads and contributes to the integration efforts described in this book is all part of bringing your teams into alignment. You need the brains, eyes and ears of different people from different parts of the organization, and you need them to be able to interact and bounce ideas off each other. However, while you want sales and marketing teams to align and integrate, it isn't the most practical thing to bring every person together for every meeting you have.

For regular coordinating between departments, five to seven is an ideal number of attendees, with no more than twelve people coming together at a time. Most of all, you need your sales and marketing leaders to head the operation, with the endorsement of any other company leadership who are responsible for making decisions. The importance of their buy-in will be underscored in chapter five. You also need representatives from both the sales and marketing teams to set aside the time and brain power to be present for planning and coordination with the other department. We show you how to decide which people belong in which meetings as well as how to organize those meetings in chapter fourteen.

When everyone in your organization understands the value of sales and marketing alignment, no matter what type of involvement they have in the actual work of it, your company achieves more and more wins. In the next chapter, we look at some of the ways your business can improve with the power of sales and marketing alignment.

Chapter 4:
Sales and Marketing Alignment Transforms Your Business

Integrate your sales and marketing teams to build the foundation for supercharged sales results.

This chapter helps you evaluate your current level of sales and marketing alignment and gives you a sneak peek at the benefits to come.

Sales and marketing teams don't always play well together; conflict occurs most often when the two teams work independently and with different objectives. While both teams might be doing the best they can in their own silos, they'll never do as well as when they remove those barriers and work together. Sales and marketing integration tears down the wall between departments and encourages greater commitment and creativity and provides forward motion for the team. It motivates teams and supercharges results by leveraging the power of teamwork. This is where the magic happens.

Sales and marketing alignment and integration are also competitive advantages. Let other companies struggle with sales and marketing conflict and poorly performing funnels. This is your opportunity to rise above your competitors.

Teams Who Work Together Win Together

We all operate under the basic idea that, for the most part, marketing teams generate leads and salespeople close deals. However, we also know (even if we don't always act like it) that when the two teams cooperate, they can score higher wins than they would on their own. Let's look at an example from one of our clients, Realtor Sales Skills, an online company that sells an educational program helping realtors improve their sales and marketing skills so they can earn more business. In the following example, the company found a creative solution through marketing and sales alignment that boosted the number of realtors who bought their program.

Realtor Sales Skills practiced one of the habits every company with aligned sales and marketing should: they had regular meetings where they shared ideas and lined up their strategies. In one meeting, Luke, the sales director, raised an issue that a traditional approach would not be able to solve: many potential customers expressed an interest in talking with someone who could speak objectively of their experiences with the Realtor Sales Skills program. Leads wanted to hear the straight story from a program alumnus—not just from online content or a salesperson.

The black-and-white model of "marketing generates leads, and sales closes deals" would make it so marketing couldn't help solve this problem at all. With siloed departments, this issue would be totally up to sales. Instead, because Realtor Sales Skills followed an aligned process, marketing came up with a solution—an ambassador program. The plan was to reach out to enthusiastic realtors who had been through the Realtor Sales Skills program and who could provide their stories as case studies, give testimonials and agree to talk to a certain number of potential customers each month.

The marketing team's contribution helped the sales team in a big way. The ambassador program accelerated their close rate significantly, an extra 10 to 20 percent. Now that leads could "de-risk" their decisions in such a concrete way, the ambassador program also sped up the average time it took for a lead to buy the program. Realtor Sales Skills' sales team had compressed time, increased confidence and improved close rates, thanks to the ingenuity of the marketing team.

Collaboration Maximizes Your Team's Lead Opportunities

The amount of time sales and marketing professionals spend on leads who aren't the right fit is staggering. The amount of time spent saying the wrong things to leads who are the right fit is just as bad.

Sales and marketing teams who work together gain a greater understanding of their leads—what those leads value, want and need. They better understand the stories those leads tell themselves about your company and its offerings. Best of all, the teams know where those leads are in their buyer's journey. **Together, integrated teams determine what information, communications and experiences best serve people on their path to becoming customers.** Sales and marketing integration also helps clarify who is the right target market for the services and products. It's the job of sales and marketing teams alike not only to know where buyers are on their journey but also to help prospects understand what they want and help them get it.

Well-integrated sales and marketing teams know and respect the company's values, visions and goals and recognize that everyone is better off for it. They understand and articulate the ways their company stands apart in the marketplace and leverage their skills to build engagement and drive value for sales leads. Their efforts are strategic and lead to a more mature sales and marketing team who can grow lead interest by encouraging qualified leads to move deeper in the funnel toward buying.

The Business Case for Sales and Marketing Integration

For sales and marketing integration to build and steadily increase momentum, an organization must do the following.

Number One: Become Aware of the Problem

Sales and marketing leadership must acknowledge that siloed sales and marketing teams achieve less than integrated teams. They must recognize that team integration benefits the organization, its customers and leads and the teams and team members themselves. They must recognize that strategy by winging it, by accident or by employing no strategy at all will not lay the groundwork for sales success.

Number Two: Accept the Need to Shift

The desired future state won't come about on its own. Leadership and the sales and marketing teams must openly advocate for team integration and prioritize it culturally and structurally. Processes and communications need to flow freely between sales and marketing. Strategic thinking, planning, process development and mapping, iteration and action are required, along with an investment in time and resources.

Number 3: Meet Buyers Where They Are on Their Buying Journey

Different types of buyers take different paths as they contemplate an offer. In an earlier example, some Realtor Sales Skills leads wanted to talk to former members of the company's educational program. Other leads evaluated whether to buy based on information such as overviews of the program itself and simple case studies. Some people are ready to buy faster than others; some research in-depth; some rely on instinct and don't research much at all. A high-performing, integrated sales and marketing team must recognize where a customer is on their buying journey to account for these different needs.

Number Four: Support Lead Movement through the Sales Funnel

Team integration involves honoring the buyer's journey continuum and moving the prospective buyer forward through the sales funnel. Leads have different wants and needs and enter the funnel at different stages. **Success in moving people through the funnel requires organization-wide commitment to guiding them from one step of their journey to the next.** The more intentional the organization's sales and marketing strategies, from initial acquisition to eventual sale, the more rewarding the results for customers, integrated teams and the organization.

Number Five: Measure Results, Iterate and Evolve

The more effectively teams come into alignment, the greater the resulting revenue performance. Sales and marketing key performance indicators (KPIs) compose the scorecard to measure the success of this alignment. This data makes it possible for teams to judge what is working well and what needs a different tactic. The combination of hard data and anecdotal evidence (quantitative and qualitative data) helps the whole team bring progress into perspective. And success begets success! When sales and marketing teams see what they can achieve together in their KPIs, they will want to align more.

How Well Aligned Is Your Sales and Marketing?

You know why sales and marketing alignment and integration are vital to the success of your business, and you're probably wondering what it takes to move forward. Before we dive into how sales and marketing integration works in practice, review the following self-assessment. This checklist summarizes how to mobilize leadership and team members to structure strategies and processes within the integrated sales funnel (all of which are described in detail in part two of this book). It will help you evaluate how your business's sales and marketing organization is now versus what you should be aiming for.

Company Leadership

- Top-level leadership understand the value of sales and marketing alignment and have made it a priority initiative for the company.

- Sales and marketing leadership and team members understand that sales and marketing alignment is a new and ongoing priority.

Team Leadership

- Leadership for both sales and marketing have revised their own job descriptions to reflect how they will work together to achieve sales and marketing alignment.

- Sales and marketing leadership agree to structure integrated sales funnels that define marketing and sales processes and tasks, team member roles and responsibilities and corresponding KPIs.

Team Players

- The members of both the sales and the marketing team have revised their job descriptions to reflect how they will cooperate with each other in the integrated sales funnel.

- Team members agree to listen to one another, providing feedback and ideas about how the processes in the integrated sales funnel can be improved.

Roles and Responsibilities in the Integrated Sales Funnel

- Sales and marketing team members have worked together to create ideal customer personas and map corresponding buyer's journeys for each one.

- Sales and marketing team members have worked together to build an integrated sales funnel that tracks each step in each agreed upon buyer's journey and each product or service offering.

- Sales and marketing team members have worked together to structure strategies and processes within the integrated sales funnel that will meet each lead where they are and guide them toward the bottom of the funnel.

- Sales and marketing team members understand their roles and responsibilities within the sales funnel and have the guidance and feedback they need to successfully execute them.

- Sales and marketing team members have determined KPIs to track for each sales process and tactic within the integrated sales funnel.

Collaboration and Feedback Loop

- Sales and marketing leadership have agreed to hold regular meetings that review data from sales and marketing activities throughout the funnel to look for places of improvement.

- Sales and marketing leadership and teams have committed to holding regular meetings to provide feedback, brainstorm and process ideas to improve sales processes and tactics within the integrated funnel.

Let's Align Sales and Marketing

Alignment and integration provide an optimal state for every company's sales and marketing team. An integrated sales and marketing team agrees to the ways in which they will work together and meet leads on their journey. They communicate the right information in the right way, at the right time, to inspire progress. They know the importance of teamwork to drive sales momentum.

All the major players at your organization need to work toward sales and marketing alignment. The top-level leadership, sales and marketing leadership and every member of the team must rally around the idea.

While conflict can kill momentum and stifle performance, sales and marketing alignment creates more positive momentum that will continue to build over time. For this reason, sales and marketing teams who play well together create exceptional value for their companies—not to mention experience greater harmony in their daily work lives!

In the chapters to follow, you will learn how to build sound sales and marketing strategies and clear, intentional processes to transform your organization and supercharge sales. We explore the steps involved in aligning the buyer's journey to an integrated sales funnel, from initial top-of-funnel engagement to middle-of-funnel interactions to bottom-of-funnel cultivated relationships. We dive deeper into leadership's role and how to get the right people in the right seats, and we help you start building the momentum you need to grow revenue sustainably.

Chapter 5:
You Get Nowhere without Buy-In from the Top

Leadership's attitudes and actions impact sales and marketing alignment.

This chapter demonstrates the ways leadership can inadvertently kill sales or be change agents to guide integration.

Before diving into sales and marketing alignment, everyone must understand that strong leadership buy-in is a must. Leadership is responsible for driving strategic vision and organizing the processes and people needed to grow sales. However, many leaders do not understand the importance of integrating sales and marketing or how to bridge these roles to maximize results, and this can often be the greatest barrier to sales growth. The following is a much-too-common scenario where top-level leadership undercut both sales and marketing success.

Leadership Perceptions Can Derail Sales and Marketing Integration

The C-level leadership team of a business has gathered to discuss troubling and declining sales numbers over the past several quarters and try to come up with ideas for how to cut costs. The chief operating officer (COO), who oversees sales, argues the company can save money by shrinking the marketing department budget and using the savings to hire more salespeople.

"Marketing is not generating sales, and the sales folks are our moneymakers," he says.

The chief information officer (CIO) has different ideas about how best to cut sales and marketing costs. She is buried deep in the new website design. Unlike the COO, she believes more marketing support is needed and the sales team can shrink once the website does a better job enticing people to buy.

"Our products will practically sell themselves," she says.

The chief financial officer (CFO) knows of a bargain-basement overseas resource who can provide sales and marketing support at 20 percent of the current budget. "They can handle SEO [search engine optimization], cold calls, email campaigns and social media posts, you name it," he says. "These guys are cheap and can do the same work."

The CIO and COO have conflicting ideas about what to prioritize, but the CEO sees a twofold opportunity to save. "With the new website and these inexpensive resources, we can slash both our marketing and our sales budgets," she says. "We'll get leaner and boost profits while we're at it."

The members of the current leadership team, who aren't necessarily experts in sales or marketing, are looking to cut expenses as opposed to investing in sales and marketing strategy, processes and people. In our experience, paring down to a skeleton crew of sales and marketing team members only adds stress and doesn't help increase revenue. Moving sales and marketing departments into alignment with one another actually increases efficiency and lowers costs.

Leadership's perceptions about sales and marketing have the potential to transform organizations and boost sales but also to drive organizations into the ground. Negative or even simply inaccurate views of the sales and marketing team's value are often the number one barrier to sales growth. Pitting sales and marketing departments against one another when it comes to human and material support does nothing to help an organization grow and thrive.

Why Leaders Shouldn't Undervalue Sales and Marketing: It's Hard Work!

Being a salesperson requires fortitude, determination and the ability to truly connect with people. Successful sales requires mastery of the company's mission, vision, differentiators and offerings, as well as lots of scheduling, systems management, tracking, training and follow-up. Salespeople must be great listeners and able to understand their prospects on many levels, so they can guide customers to purchase their company's offering.

Marketing is responsible for the first impressions most people get of a company, and they are instrumental in whether a lead decides to move further down the sales funnel. They need to capture attention and hold a lead's interest by establishing a brand presence, handling graphic design, creating content, building a website that sells, managing social media profiles and creating successful ads and promotions. Investing in good marketing is integral to making positive impressions on would-be customers throughout their buyer's journey.

When strong and capable sales and marketing team members come together, their combined strengths make a company look and perform its best, from the moment a lead becomes aware of it to the moment the same lead becomes a customer.

How Leadership Can Kill Sales and Marketing Alignment

Leadership sets the stage, the focus and the pace for a sales and marketing team. A leadership team's perceptions, presumptions, value and vision can make or break their company's sales and marketing results.

Answering the following questions will provide a starting place for leadership's perceptions of sales and marketing and how their support or lack of support impacts results.

- How does leadership acknowledge and model positive perceptions of sales and marketing throughout the organization?

- In what ways does leadership work to inspire the sales and marketing team as well as cultivate and elevate their day-to-day efforts?

- How are sales achievements managed and rewarded?

Many leaders struggle with trusting their sales and marketing teams. It can be tough for some leaders to allow the space that a healthy sales and marketing team requires to co-create and fine-tune processes and tactics—they may be tempted to dictate what needs to be done from the top down. That approach means companies miss out on creative solutions that their teams can come up with when they put their heads together. It can also erode trust and team happiness, which definitely has a negative effect on sales performance.

Micromanaging teams is also inefficient. Imagine our orchestra from chapter one, which contains dozens of people playing different instruments. Sometimes the string instruments, wind instruments and brass instruments like to separate into sections and practice together on their own without the conductor, so they can play their parts more competently when they come back together. Now imagine if the orchestra conductor made a rule against these sections practicing without the conductor watching them. That would limit every player's ability to strengthen their skills and be confident in their contribution to the group. **Trusting teams to do their own work and then stepping in to lead when the time comes results in more skilled and confident performers, which helps teams work in harmony and get better results for the company.**

That is not to say a leader should be completely hands-off. They still need to be involved in the work of sales and marketing. Leaders who don't share their business strategy or provide guidance around vision and processes hold back these teams from reaching their potential. They must also train and help the team build their skills, set clear goals and then get out of their way so the team can do the revenue-building work they were hired to do. Without this intentionality, leaders may be killing sales without meaning to.

There are two types of leaders who, if they are not careful, can kill sales. The first has a strong sales and marketing background, and the second has little training or understanding of sales and marketing. Neither state is inherently bad, but either of them can go wrong.

Leaders with Strong Sales and Marketing Backgrounds

These energetic, charismatic leaders excelled at the sales and marketing work that launched their careers or grew their companies. They value sales and marketing expertise, processes and funnels (at least in theory) because they have lived it. But star quarterbacks don't always (or even usually) make great coaches. Similarly, while superstar salespeople may be charismatic and passionate about sales, their passion may not transfer to managing day-to-day operations and overseeing sales funnels.

Leaders with strong sales and marketing backgrounds tend to create sales-driven organizations; however, they may lean too heavily toward either sales or marketing, depending on their background, and they may not understand the benefits of integrating the sales and marketing teams. Often leaders who are successful at sales or marketing have a difficult time developing a team to replicate their personal successes.

Leaders without Sales and Marketing Backgrounds

Leaders who come from a background other than sales and marketing often devalue the importance of both, due either to lack of understanding or too much of an emphasis on the products and services selling themselves.

Think of the C-level executives from earlier in this chapter. Cost-cutting attitudes like the ones they displayed can manifest in a lot of different ways. A CFO may see marketing as a commodity or expense rather than an investment toward the company's growth. As a result, some of the marketing support the CFO hires may be cheap, check-the-box resources. The CFO may also have unrealistic short-term expectations of sales and marketing teams and return on investment (ROI). A COO, in turn, may see all salespeople as interchangeable cogs in the corporate wheel and may not value or optimize the specialized teams and individuals who can help them stabilize and grow revenue. By only considering the costs of these departments (and how they can cut those costs), both executives overlook the opportunities for growth and positive outcomes that come from sales and marketing alignment.

These leadership attributes can be difficult to overcome and often require a mindset change. This is where the concepts in this book can be used to educate and enlighten leaders to more concretely understand how to invest and support effective sales and marketing strategies.

Signs That Leadership Are Killing Sales

The way business leaders think about sales and marketing drives the way they lead. Obviously, if members of leadership see marketing as a necessary evil and salespeople as overpaid employees who need to "just sell more," it's a sign that they don't understand the real value of sales and marketing. Sometimes the signs are a little more subtle, though.

Here are a few signs that leadership need a mindset shift when it comes to sales and marketing:

- Leaders build or reinforce a corporate culture that undervalues sales and marketing efforts.

- They don't see the point of spending money on sales and marketing initiatives and instead cut budgets and personnel for those departments.

- They choose quick-fix revenue solutions instead of strengthening foundations and building a sales and marketing organization based on strategy and processes.

- They argue against investing in integrated technology solutions and platforms to bridge sales and marketing team efforts and raise everyone's game.

- They perceive individual team members as commodities instead of working to understand their strengths and investing the time necessary to facilitate their growth.

Leaders who do not understand sales and marketing might be resistant to spending money on a marketing budget or on hiring experienced professionals for the team. They may think that anyone can do marketing—just have the IT guy handle the website and the receptionist post on the Facebook page. The CEO's niece is learning graphic design at the community college, so they'll just have her design that new brochure for free rather than hiring a contractor.

Unsupportive leaders are often impatient with sales processes and funnels. Especially if they're in a more old-school mindset, they may think that sales are low because their team members simply aren't spending enough time on the phone. They also tend to view their salespeople as entitled and believe they're paid too much and their commissions should be capped.

Maybe you have observed these types of actions and words from your leadership team, or maybe you have even held some of these attitudes yourself. If so, thanks for continuing to read! You're already on your way to a mindset shift, and having this information will help you do better. Change starts with an awareness of biases and areas where the leader's vision may be impeded.

The good news is that with heightened awareness comes the opportunity to realign and refocus by taking well-defined actions.

Leaders as Sales and Marketing Change Agents

For healthy revenue, leaders must recognize the critical role they play in accelerating organizational change and inspiring those around them to see the world the way they do. Leaders should become sales and marketing change agents, setting the stage for a more methodical, intentional route forward instead of pursuing a series of random tactics or looking for quick wins. The following are not methodical, intentional strategies:

"Let's find cheap resources to do what our agency does!"
"Let's post more often on social media!"
"Let's redesign our website!"
"Let's make more cold calls!"
"Let's steal great salespeople away from a competitor!"

They are quick fixes and do not drive overnight success. In fact, you probably won't have much success at all with these tactics.

Once leadership undergoes a mindset shift to value sales and marketing teams, they can model that valuation for the rest of the company and optimize their insights. They can foster the integration of a high-performing sales and marketing team and invest in and manage that team as a revenue-producing asset. They can pave the way for a strategically designed, intentional sales engine with clear roles, clear processes, clear sales and marketing activities and clear KPIs. They can stabilize revenue ups and downs and achieve increasingly ambitious growth targets. The bottom line is this: leaders are responsible for driving these necessary changes.

How Leaders Guide Teams to Success

Leaders must look internally for the root causes of their organization's problems. They must build the foundations necessary to align team members, inspire others to share the company vision, break apart silos and collaborate in order to achieve bigger and bigger wins. The leader must pinpoint where they want to go and then build a strategy the entire team can rally around.

Consider the following ways leaders can improve sales and marketing team performance.

Show Respect

Sales and marketing experts know how to identify prospects' pain points and offer targeted solutions that guide them down the sales funnel. These efforts require determination, passion, hard work and a valuable skill set honed over time. Leaders must demonstrate that they understand how sales and marketing directly contribute to the company's mission, vision, goals and ultimate success. When leaders value their efforts and show them respect, the team will give everything they've got and help achieve even the most ambitious revenue goals.

Support Teamwork

To boost sales team performance, sales and marketing experts need to work together. The problem is that they often work in silos. What they can do alone pales in comparison to what they can do by combining forces. It's the leader's job to define team goals and align teams toward a common vision.

Ask for Feedback and Pay Attention

The best way to uncover sales and marketing roadblocks is to ask questions. If the team isn't performing as well as expected, the leader should ask what they think is going on. The leaders can ask what prospects and customers want and what's preventing deals from closing. The leader must rely on the sales team to be the eyes and ears of the company.

Promote and Drive Ongoing Integrated Training

Whether it's about using a new lead database, or CRM, or a new way of automating emails or seeking sales skills, sales and marketing team members can attend training workshops as a team to integrate learning. We recommend removing training silos in sales and marketing and bringing the teams together for both marketing and sales training sessions.

Focus on Results and Watch the Numbers

As they come into alignment, sales and marketing team members will be asked to track KPIs for the sales and marketing processes over which they have taken ownership. While they will regularly check in with one another regarding those numbers and how they can be improved, it's the responsibility of leaders to regularly and methodically review these KPIs within the greater scope of the company's goals. This oversight allows leaders to accurately determine where a strategy can be improved and who would benefit most from constructive feedback. Micromanaging is inefficient, but sales and marketing teams still need to know what they are working toward and get support from leadership on strategy and execution.

At the end of the day, sales team performance relates directly to understanding, respect, empowerment, engagement and support from leadership. **By encouraging the strengths of individual sales and marketing team members, leaders can cultivate a healthier workplace environment, promote employee engagement and improve sales and marketing performance.** The more aligned, empowered and energized your sales and marketing teams, the faster real change occurs and the more likely that change sticks. It all comes back to a strong vision, collaborative teaming and intentional progress toward a new desired state.

Celebrate Wins and Have Fun

It's no surprise that sales and marketing teams can be compared to sports teams—a team's efforts can result in visible, measurable success. There are many ways to score points in sales and marketing (which we dive into later in this book). Because of these opportunities to count wins, you also have opportunities to acknowledge the work of your team and celebrate in ways that make everyone feel appreciated. Taking a moment to look at what you are doing right is great for team morale and encourages future success.

The Leadership Process for Thriving Marketing and Sales Teams

Once a leader understands the efforts and expertise of their marketing and sales teams, their job becomes to drive the strategy and allocate people, resources and the time to meet sales goals. Following is the process a successful leader follows to integrate sales and marketing teams and harness their skills for success.

A Leader's Mindset Sets the Tone

Developing an appreciation for the work of sales and marketing is an important start to a shift in attitude that could change the entire way your organization operates. When a leader recognizes sales and marketing integration as a priority and rallies everyone around the idea, that mindset starts to manifest into action.

Staying true to the need for team integration may be one of the most important decisions leaders will make. However, the inevitable improvements will not happen overnight, and will never happen if the leader does not walk the talk. A sustained commitment to a new paradigm takes planning, alignment, integration and support within and between teams, and that requires support from up top.

Often a CEO will come into a meeting, announce their new priorities and then walk away, expecting they will return to the massive change they've envisioned. Without concrete, consistent support to sales and marketing, that won't happen. Instead, it will end in frustration for all involved.

Sales results take time, and there is a risk that leaders may abandon the team integration process and return to business as usual. However, when they do hold that vision and hold space for sales and marketing to begin coordinating their efforts, that's when the magic can start happening.

Leaders Must Overcome Internal Barriers

Leaders set the tone for cooperation between sales and marketing. Unfortunately, that tone is sometimes negative. Some leaders take for granted that one department is more important than another due to their past work experience. Others are used to automatically blaming the other department for not setting them up for success, and they default to finger pointing whenever sales dip.

We have seen sales and marketing leaders clash with one another for fear of being blamed for any revenue shortcomings. In one case, we witnessed a marketing manager strongly resisting a request from sales to share metrics and make projections regarding how many leads they could bring in—he was concerned that if he made the wrong call he would be "in trouble." For him, being asked to share numbers or make predictions was a trigger to go on the defensive, possibly held over from previous negative sales and marketing interactions in his career.

As far as he was concerned, his duty was to maintain branding and content that aligned to the marketing department's internal standards. As long as he could apply brand consistency across all channels, success would follow.

Leaders must be the first to overcome their own biases to model cooperation and not fall prey to historical triggers. If you as a sales or marketing leader are placing the blame on the other department, your team will likely follow suit, and that will diminish your chances of success. Make sure you're the person building the bridge; if you do it right, that bridge will more easily bear the weight of everyone on the team to cross together.

Leaders Push through with Strategy, Processes and People

Acting on a new shift in mindset means committing and recommitting to holding the space and structure that will allow sales and marketing to thrive. That means encouraging their people to develop and tune their strategy and processes. We talk more about those strategies and processes in the next chapter.

Leaders must be willing to give time and financial support to their team so they can develop integrated strategies, ensuring the right processes are in place and getting the right people on board. Not only must they offer material support but regularly communicate their vision with their words and actions to make it more likely this new approach will take root. This will result in major rewards for the leader, the team and the company.

The Rewards of Leading an Integrated Team

There's a lot to look forward to when leaders support an integrated sales and marketing organization. For one thing, the team becomes more autonomous. Having strategies in place defines everyone's roles and responsibilities. There are built-in ways for teams to monitor their own progress and recognize opportunities to improve. That means leaders can spend less time grasping for silver bullets that may end up being ineffective at best and defective at worst.

Additionally, this level of success and empowerment usually raises team morale and unity. When your company culture is healthier and your people feel valued, they approach their work with more intentionality, and that's good for the company's bottom line. It's also a competitive advantage in a highly competitive business world.

Next Steps for Leaders Willing to Integrate Sales and Marketing

You now know what you're aiming for when you integrate your sales and marketing organization. Preparing yourself to set and oversee this vision starts with taking stock of where you are right now.

Evaluate Your Own Attitudes and Behavior

Leaders, including managers and team leads, should start by looking inward to see if you're blocking your team's success. Do you or any of your colleagues believe the sales and marketing teams are lazy and negligent? Do you theoretically support sales and marketing without committing to consistent practical and moral support?

Ask yourself the following questions. Are you, as your organization's leader, willing to...

1. Commit to, support and prioritize sales and marketing alignment?

2. Prioritize resources and people to take ownership of strategies, tactics and actions?

3. Seek to understand and learn from the sales and marketing teams?

4. Create a safe place to explore ideas and empower teams to move forward?

5. Recognize that the process requires ongoing commitment versus a quick fix?

The good news is, if you (the leader) are the problem, it's easier for you to be the problem solver. It can be hard to admit to oneself you are responsible for your company's sales slump. However, leaders who ask the hard questions and accept changes can build happier, more loyal teams with higher performance.

Walk in the Shoes of Your Sales and Marketing Teams

Leaders must remember to listen to your teams. It does not hurt to spend some time walking in their shoes and getting closer to their actual work to relate to them. To foster a safer, more collaborative environment, a leader must encourage team members to share input and must themselves model respect to the rest of the team as you listen to the answer.

Most marketing and sales professionals are good at what they do, so long as they feel their work is relevant and they have the opportunity to sell the way that best supports their strengths. The leader is responsible for putting each team member in the right role and creating an environment for them to be successful as individuals and all together.

This understanding is at the heart, and is the first step, to developing sales and marketing integration.

Build Bridges, Not Fences, for Sales and Marketing Teams

Sales and marketing teams can blame each other for shortcomings, or they can channel their energy to acknowledge the underlying causes of the revenue problems the organization is facing. Leadership plays a major role in reducing conflict to build sales momentum. You must help the sales and marketing teams see collaboration as a nonnegotiable priority, paramount along with setting integrated strategies and processes with clear owners. Leadership can build or reinforce a culture that recognizes and rewards higher-performing teams whose strong foundation and collective efforts result in more impressive ROI and stronger sales.

Conflict is a brick wall that kills momentum and stifles performance. The key to getting over that wall is to identify the misunderstandings that interfere with sales and marketing integration and then create an environment where the root problems can be addressed head-on to foster alignment and create real change from both the top down and the bottom up.

Action Steps for Business Leaders and Leadership Teams

- Consider your preconceived notions about sales and marketing tasks and your perceptions of your marketing staff and sales-people. Does your mindset help grow sales, or is it a roadblock?

- Ask your team what additional support or resources they could use and how exactly those will impact growth.

- Spend time understanding the key roles of your sales and marketing teams. Some ways to do this include listening and taking part in sales calls, assisting in writing marketing copy and sitting down with your team members to ask them about the work they do daily. Learn the strengths and weaknesses of your sales and marketing teams and place them in roles where they will be the most successful.

- Guide teams by showing respect and trust, supporting team-work (without micromanaging), soliciting and listening to feedback from team members, encouraging and facilitating ongoing skills training, focusing on results and celebrating wins together. Mentor your team by celebrating their successes both individually and as a team, coaching them in areas of opportunity and encouraging them when they are struggling.

Chapter 6:

Strategy Provides Direction and Guidance to Sales and Marketing Alignment

Determine where you are today and set the right direction for where you want to be in the future.

This chapter shows you how an aligned strategy provides the framework needed to build processes and introduces the Revenue Equation diagnostic to help you get started.

When you want to hit a target, the process is simple. First, you get ready; then, you aim; finally, you fire. The process of executing a sales and marketing strategy should be just as methodical; get ready by laying down foundations for your sales and marketing teams, get clear on what audience you are targeting and then pull the trigger to execute your plan.

The problem is that many sales and marketing teams skip the first two steps and go right to pulling the trigger on key decisions. For example, they may slap together a Google Ads campaign without aligning keywords and copy for the ads with what is being offered on their company landing page (or they just send people to a home page where the connection to the Google Ad isn't clear). For a tactic to work, a plan must first be in place to justify it; success in sales and marketing starts with strategy.

Earlier in this book, we defined *strategy* as the overarching game plan that sets the direction in which you want to head. In this chapter, we discuss how to create the right strategies to effectively guide your sales and marketing teams. To start, you need to take three key steps:

1. Establish where you are.

2. Determine where you want to go.

3. Do a gap analysis to plan how you'll get there. We show you how to do that analysis and how to act on it in the coming chapters.

Your company's strategy ultimately determines the success of your sales and marketing efforts, which in turn determines whether you hit your company's revenue and profitability goals. **The ability to identify strengths, weaknesses, areas of misalignment, easy adjustments and other steps provides both direction and visibility into the sales and marketing integration journey.** The best tool we have to get this done is the Revenue Equation.

Setting the Stage for a Winning Strategy: The Revenue Equation

An effective strategy comprises intentional steps that enable you to achieve well-defined, measurable sales goals. If you were to go from department to department within a company, asking people to define the company's foundations, they probably would not say the same thing as one another. In fact, they may not have anything to say at all. Without the entire organization (including departments outside of sales and marketing such as operations and delivery) coming to a shared understanding of who the company is, what its offerings are and who its ideal customers are, the sales and marketing strategy will not be nearly as effective as it could be.

The Revenue Equation is a framework for sales and marketing organizations based on understanding the root causes of sales and marketing problems, then creating systems to solve them. Karl developed this equation as well as associated tools to help clients build a high-performing sales and marketing organization and improve revenue performance. **Once leadership teams, managers and sales and marketing teams understand the Revenue Equation, the root causes and corresponding actionable solutions to sales and marketing problems become clear.** When everyone in a company has a common understanding of what needs to happen to go forward, teamwork strengthens and the team functions more effectively.

The equation consists of three factors that, when added together, lead to equal revenue stabilization and growth.

- **Foundations:** Who you are and how you communicate your value

- **Design:** Who you sell to and their unique buyer's journey

- **Infrastructure:** The strategy, people and processes required to fulfill your design for each customer

Following is an overview of what you will be determining for each factor of your Revenue Equation.

Components of the Revenue Equation Factors		
Foundations + Design + Infrastructure = Revenue Stabilization and Growth		
Foundations	**Design**	**Infrastructure**
Value Proposition Key Differentiators Customer Experience Promise Foundational Messaging	Target Audience Characteristics Ideal Customer Personas The Buyer's Journey Selling Tactics and Assets	Team Roles and Responsibilities Sales Process Sales and Marketing Technology Sales Forecasting and KPIs Performance Management

Using the Revenue Equation

The first step in determining what kind of work you need to do is to identify your problem areas, the places where your leaders and the rest of your sales and marketing teams aren't aligning. That's why we've provided an assessment called the Revenue Equation to help you determine how marketing and sales teams are currently working and identify where misfires and malfunctions are happening. It enables teams to evaluate their organization through the lens of each factor in the Revenue Equation. (You can also access the Revenue Equation diagnostic tool at revenueequation.com.)

Once your team aligns on areas for improvement, you can begin to fix what's broken in order to stabilize operations and enable further growth.

Sales and Marketing Foundations

In one way or another, every person at your company is a salesperson. Each person represents the company in their interactions with the outside world. However, if the marketing and sales teams (and all the rest of the employees) don't know what your company does and why, you're creating risks and potentially leaving money on the table. The following should be well-defined and understood within your organization to best determine an effective strategy. Have everyone in your organization fill out the following assessment to see how aligned you are right now.

On a scale of low to high, how well DEFINED and UNDERSTOOD is each of the following within your organization?	1= Low 10 = High
Problems We Solve: The root problems that your organization solves	1 2 3 4 5 6 7 8 9 10
Value Proposition: The way you create value and deliver that value to your clients	1 2 3 4 5 6 7 8 9 10
Key Differentiators: The attributes that clearly separate you from the competition	1 2 3 4 5 6 7 8 9 10
Customer Experience Promise: The defined experiences you want to create for your clients	1 2 3 4 5 6 7 8 9 10
Offerings: The products and/or services your company provides its customers	1 2 3 4 5 6 7 8 9 10
Average Score	

Getting clarity and agreement from all team members regarding the foundational elements of your company is essential to your success. Once you do, you'll be able to identify and communicate your competitive advantages both inside and outside your organization. Your best prospects will connect with these values and be drawn to your company as a result. Designing a system to determine who these prospects may be is your next step.

Sales and Marketing Design

Sales and marketing design defines who a company sells to and the buyer's journey starting from a lead's awareness of the company to closed business. The following should be well-defined and understood within your organization. Have everyone in your organization fill out the following assessment to see how aligned you are right now.

On a scale of low to high, how well DEFINED and USED is each of the following within your organization?	1= Low 10 = High
Target Audience Organization: The types of organizations that purchase your offerings	1 2 3 4 5 6 7 8 9 10
Ideal Customer Persona: A hypothetical person suited to purchase your offerings	1 2 3 4 5 6 7 8 9 10
Buyer's Journey: A series of steps buyers go through that represents the purchasing lifecycle	1 2 3 4 5 6 7 8 9 10
Campaigns: Defined strategies and tactics to bring buyers into and through the sales funnel	1 2 3 4 5 6 7 8 9 10
Average Score	

Most sales and marketing professionals are clear on their target audiences. The teams know how they're supposed to show up for their leads and their customers. Where it gets hairy is when teams go to align the steps a seller needs to take to intersect with the buyer's journey. Many teams don't really know what steps their customers take from entering the funnel to deciding to buy, which makes it impossible for them to create a strategy for meeting them where they are.

Sales design is the process of determining what a buyer's journey is and mapping the ideal customer persona's movement through each stage of the sales funnel. Once you do that, the next set of tasks uses this map to create a strategy and plan every step to accelerate your leads through each stage of the funnel.

Sales and Marketing Infrastructure

After aligning your understanding of your foundations, designing your ideal customer personas and mapping their journeys, it's time to address infrastructure. Not surprisingly, sales infrastructure and processes are usually where organizations are the shakiest, and they're least likely to provide aligned answers to this portion of the Revenue Equation—if they can do so at all!

Analysis of your marketing and sales infrastructure determines if companies have refined processes and if each step in those processes has a clear owner. The following should be well-defined and understood within your organization. Have everyone in your organization fill out the following assessment to see how aligned you are right now.

On a scale of low to high, how well DEFINED and USED is each of the following within your organization?	1= Low 10 = High
Roles and Responsibilities: Defined ownership of activities within each stage of the sales funnel	1 2 3 4 5 6 7 8 9 10
Sales Process: Structured actions required to cultivate a prospect from lead stage to close	1 2 3 4 5 6 7 8 9 10
Sales and Marketing Technology: Tech used to increase sales funnel efficiency and effectiveness	1 2 3 4 5 6 7 8 9 10
Sales Forecasting and KPIs: Data used to evaluate team and sales funnel performance	1 2 3 4 5 6 7 8 9 10

On a scale of low to high, how well DEFINED and USED is each of the following within your organization?	1= Low 10 = High
Performance Management: Process to optimize the sales and marketing organization	1 2 3 4 5 6 7 8 9 10
Average Score	

Each of these elements needs to be known by every leader and member of the sales and marketing team. Coming into alignment may take some time, but once you do, you will have laid the vital groundwork for creating effective sales and marketing strategies and all the steps that they comprise.

How Your Revenue Equation Leads to Strategic Success

Strategy development is no easy feat; however, having a bad strategy (or no strategy at all) is dangerous and inhibits a company's ability to achieve desired results. Refining the Revenue Equation—sales and marketing foundations, design and infrastructure—creates accountability, increases efficiency and optimizes performance. **Once sales and marketing teams develop clarity around their company's Revenue Equation, they can work together to fill in the gaps it reveals.**

Through doing the work laid out in the following chapters, your team will learn to define an ideal customer profile, then develop processes and tactics to bring a lead into and through the sales funnel to the point of buying. In the following chapters, we get into more details on the buyer's journey, developing sales funnels and the processes and tactics to match.

Action Items

- Administer the Revenue Equation to your leaders and those in your sales and marketing teams. This creates a starting point from where your company can regard each part of the Revenue Equation, which in turn will create visibility and alignment. This yields conversations across the team, together, about where to focus resources to build stronger foundations from which to grow strategy. Use the tools in this book or revenueequation.com.

- As a group, brainstorm, discuss and come to an agreement regarding your company's sales and marketing foundations. Especially focus on how your company creates value, how you create this value better than your competitors, the specifics and details of your offerings and the experience you want every lead and customer to have when they interact with anyone at your company.

- Read on to learn more about creating strategies for sales and marketing design and infrastructure that maximize the efforts of both departments and that lead to revenue sustainability and growth.

Chapter 7:
Determining Your Ideal Customer and Charting the Buyer's Journey

Knowing what motivates ideal customers to move through the integrated sales funnel is essential to closing sales.

This chapter teaches you how to develop precise personas for your ideal customers and design a persona's buyer's journey detailing their current state, the way they evaluate risks and solutions and the factors that influence their decisions to buy.

In our consulting and training work, we often encounter clients who are confident they know their ideal customer very well. When we ask who and for more details, they may say something like "We sell to tech companies." Often, that is as specific as their definition gets.

It's a great start, but the understanding needs to go deeper to who has a say in the decision-making and who exactly makes the decision to purchase. To really get a meaningful understanding of a customer, sales and marketing teams must craft a nuanced individual persona of whoever makes buying decisions at a given company. They should ask as many questions as possible related to what the buyer's life is like, what challenges they encounter, what their life will look like if they purchase a company's solution and how they evaluate and determine what solution to purchase in the end.

Staying at the surface level of who a customer is results in gaps in the sales and marketing team's knowledge and effectiveness. Misunderstandings easily flood into those gaps and make messes of sales and marketing processes and messaging. They end up with incomplete strategies where a lead either doesn't enter the sales funnel at all or stalls out inside of it; whether it's one or the other, the customer won't end up buying.

It is equally ineffective when everybody on an integrated team has a completely different idea of who they are supposed to be talking to, and high-level labels can equal vague definitions open to misinterpretation. *Tech company* might mean "SaaS" to your marketing director and "IT service provider" to your sales director. That lack of alignment will result in a big difference between your messaging, offering and the way you seek out and interact with customers. It also means that the marketing content you create will be all over the place. When your ideal customer does come along, they may look at the content you've provided and say, "I have no idea whether this is for me." Misalignment causes major inefficiencies and errors in effectiveness of integrated sales and marketing campaigns, and that makes real risks and financial mistakes more common.

Building a sales strategy means creating multiple processes that guide your leads, from the moment they become interested in your product or service to when your sales team closes business with them. **To create those processes and the touchpoints along the way, it is sales and marketing's job to chart a path that your ideal customer can see laid out in front of them and easily follow.** Everyone on your team needs to know who the customer is and have consistent information that helps their decision-making process. You need to have the scripts and content to answer their questions before they even know what to ask, and you need to understand what they will be thinking before they do. This is where the magic happens and where significant sales performance can be generated.

The Value of Knowing Your Customer

Understanding your buyers and adapting to the real concerns they exhibit is a practical step for both the marketing and the sales teams. It changes the content that marketing creates, the conversations salespeople have with leads and the way the buyer is moved toward a purchase. Here is an example of that concept in practice.

Karl was working with a professional services firm that was sending leads to a landing page listing their offerings and asking them to complete an interest form. They could see a decent number of visitors to the web page but were confused as to why none of the leads were completing the interest form or reaching out with a phone call. From what they saw in Google Analytics, the ads that were drawing people to the page seemed effective. But the visitors weren't taking action once they got to the page.

From looking at the data, Karl and the client deduced that the landing page itself wasn't working the way they wanted. It had to be the messaging that was turning leads off from wanting to learn more. They concluded that they were asking for too big of a leap—there was a missing piece between visiting the landing page and filling out the form. The sales and marketing team needed to learn more about the customer to figure out what that piece was.

Without truly understanding their buyers, sales and marketing departments will have a difficult time solving problems like that one. Here is the system Karl designed for creating these hyper-specific ideal customer personas and detailed buyer's journeys that help integrated sales and marketing teams craft content.

Organize and Rank Your Customers

The first step to drilling down from a broad category like *tech company* to something more specific is to start with who you already sell to. Get input from both sales and marketing to evaluate your current customers. Start by listing all your customers' market segments and separating them in a way that best suits the way your company does business, whether that means by industry, yearly revenue, company demographics or the criteria they use to make buying decisions. If you have many kinds of customers, cut the list to no more than ten categories (though three to five is ideal) so you can identify big-picture trends and commonalities between the customers you like to work with. This enables you to be precise when you develop specific messaging that best relates to each group, causing your sales and marketing efforts to generate more sales.

Narrow Your List to Your Top Customer Types

Categorizing your customers gives insights into what they have in common, but if your sales and marketing team wants to get laser-focused on what customers want, you need to refine your thinking even further. Your business only has so many resources to dedicate to sales and marketing efforts, so spend them on as many valuable leads as possible.

You might know right away who your best customers are, but it helps to have criteria to know for sure whether they will help you meet the goals you have for your business. This next level of intentionality will support you and your team as you chart your strategy for sales growth. We like to consider the following qualities.

- **Profitability:** Whether the customer is marginally profitable or too expensive to provide any more value or, worse, whether they cause your company to lose money. Look at what percentage of your yearly revenue they account for, current and forecasted lifetime value, typical margins, etc.

- **Headache:** Whether having a greater number of these types of customers will create more headaches for you and your team than they are worth (e.g., they often call you in a panic, your team dreads working with them, etc.). Remember, when you seek out customers the right way, you can attract the ones you really want.

- **Enjoyment:** Whether this customer is pleasant to work with (e.g., your missions and visions align, they are open to feedback, you can imagine hanging out with them outside of work, etc.). While this criterion may seem like a luxury, we have found some of the best clients are not only fun and positive to work with but also refer other clients, have lifetime financial value and are often some of the most profitable accounts.

To choose which of these three categories matters to you the most, ask what your company is aiming for and consider its goals and values. If you own a family business where work-life balance is a high priority, you might weigh high enjoyment and low headache over the most profitable (yet possibly high-maintenance) customers. If you want to make a lot of money fast so you can sell your business and move on, you might decide to keep taking headache customers who pay a lot of money. This is not an exact science, but using this approach is often an effective strategy to bring you the customers you really want.

Find Your Way to Your Ideal Buyer

Now that you have your customer types rated, it's time to zoom in further to the type of specific people at these companies who would buy your offering, down to their job title and the everyday struggles they face. How would you discover that ideal customer and then communicate with them in a way they resonate with? Figuring out the buyer's journey for your ideal customer is a journey in itself, one full of hypothesizing and testing but one that is extremely important to the future success of your sales and marketing initiatives.

To continue our earlier example, instead of saying your customers are tech companies, you could refine your target further by saying, "I'm selling to the VP of engineering at a midsize software company whose development team does not have enough people or the critical skills to get a product to market in time." This added level of detail allows your sales and marketing organization to get super clear on your ideal customer and opens the door to more effective and creative ways of attracting and interacting with the best leads for your business.

When Your Ideal Buyer Needs Something You Didn't Foresee

When Karl started working with Benjamin, the CEO of software development company MaxDevPartners, their first goal was to clarify what the company had to offer to solve their customer's problems. In this case, MaxDevPartners provided developers; these people helped their customers augment or expand their software development capabilities, so they could build software products more effectively. MaxDevPartners had on staff lots of software developers with different expertise. So, Benjamin's offer was based on providing customers with agile software development teams that could either integrate with the client's own teams or build products autonomously.

Just as we have suggested, Benjamin started his journey to finding his ideal customer persona by understanding his past and current customers. Then he asked himself the question: who could use additional software developers to level-up their current team or put their software product on the fast track? Based on his current customer list, Benjamin hypothesized two different customer types: early-stage funded companies who needed to bring a product to market quickly and more mature companies who needed additional development capacity and expertise to meet product deadlines and business initiatives.

Starting from there, Benjamin's team built a list of companies in these two categories with job openings that aligned with the type of developers MaxDevPartners offered, so they could introduce these companies to their solutions. Now that Benjamin had a good idea of who their ideal customer was, he was ready to test out whether his hypothesis was correct.

MaxDevPartners' sales and marketing team developed messaging they thought would resonate the most with these two potential audiences and crafted a series of emails and landing page copy clearly aligned with what those emails said. Then they got to work, customizing the emails to each lead on the list they built. Along the way, they tracked data, looking at open rates and click rates from the links in the emails to the landing page and website traffic. They called leads who were going to the landing pages to more formally introduce the company.

The marketing team found certain subject lines and messages performed better than others at bringing the leads to the website. However, when the sales team followed up with calls and more personalized emails, they reported that the audiences weren't interested in the team solution being promoted on the website. MaxDevPartners' offer to provide an autonomous team of developers was based on what their long-term customers were buying. New leads were not interested in teams. Instead, they wanted to hire individual developers. They simply felt the risk of outsourcing to a team was too much of a risk, that they would lose control of the development process.

Benjamin's company was used to the agile software development methodology, where companies run short sprints, fail fast and learn and adapt quickly. This meant Benjamin could swiftly pivot and use the sales team's discoveries to reshape this campaign. Instead of teams, MaxDevPartners began to offer individual developers who could hit the ground running and work alongside the customer's own teams to build products.

Based on a better understanding of their customer, the next series of outreach emails had new messaging focusing on a series of offering configurations that aligned to what his sales team had learned. As you may have guessed, the evolved messaging showed higher open rates, earned higher click rates and provided more leads that converted to sales. Pinpointing the needs of their target customers and learning what was important to them changed the game.

While you carefully think about constructing your own ideal customer personas and their buyer's journeys, pay attention to what is happening around you. Be sure to allow for flexibility and communication between sales and marketing team members as you design and adjust. Be especially sensitive to the risk points that leads express concern over (in the case of MaxDevPartners' leads, the prospect of losing control over their software development processes). Your ability to sell your offerings to them depends on your ability to address those risks.

Paint a Picture of Your Ideal Customer Persona

Ideal customer personas are semifictional representations of your ideal customers. Creating these personas helps you identify the checkpoints buyers pass through on their journeys from their current state to a purchase. By understanding the characteristics of each persona, sales and marketing teams communicate the benefits of your offering more effectively to your target audiences, meeting them where they are on their own specific journey.

Building an ideal customer persona prompts sales and marketing professionals to dig in and understand the nuances of what the people who buy from you are really thinking about. When the entire sales and marketing team is familiar with the persona, it becomes much easier for marketing to build content that leads will appreciate and for sales to anticipate the risks leads may perceive and the objections they may have to buying their company's solutions.

Introducing the Ideal Customer Persona

When you create a persona for the person you will sell to, you should try to make it as realistic and detailed as possible, down to choosing a fictional name and matching stock photo. We find thinking about a current customer who can represent your ideal target persona is a good way to get started since this customer is real and you can apply historic, real-world information. Building these personas by interviewing your customers and talking to your sales team leads to a more accurate understanding of the checkpoints leads pass through on their way to eventually purchasing from you.

PERSONAL DEMOGRAPHICS

Start by imagining the ideal customer persona's **profile and general characteristics**.

- **Name:** Dream up first, last, maybe even middle initial. You're of course not looking for an ideal name in a customer, but giving this representative persona a complete name will help you stay focused on them as a fully imagined example.

- **Typical job title or titles:** We recommend no more than five, with three being ideal.

- **Age range:** An approximation is fine.

- **Gender:** Choose according to the general patterns you have seen for a given job title among your existing customers.

- **Additional or secondary job titles:** This can be the spillover from the typical job titles; use bullet points if you need to include more than five.

- **How long the person has been at their company:** There may be triggers based on the ideal customer persona's tenure that indicate when you should approach them, what risks they are focused on and what concerns you may need to address.

- **Their past education and work experience:** There may be similarities between ideal customers when it comes to these key points too. For example, you may find that your best customers have advanced degrees in a specific subject.

- **Content they consume:** Knowing how your persona consumes content will help you know where to find them. These include websites they visit, blogs, books or publications they read, influencers they listen to and events they attend.

- **Any other indicators of personality and priorities:** Examples include marital status, number of kids, pets or even hobbies. While this last point might seem unnecessary, we have found that our own clients often share these "other" attributes. For example, we have found that business owners who are in professional development organizations like Vistage International are more comfortable with hiring outside consultants (like us) to augment their strategy development, execution and teams.

Sample Ideal Customer Persona

Jonathan Frasier is a vice president of engineering at a midsize software company with an average development team of ten to twenty developers. He has a technical background and has been at the company for three to five years as part of the leadership team and has been part of the company as they have experienced rapid growth. Typical annual revenue is $20–50 million. He's a nontraditional engineer—meaning he doesn't just know how to design and troubleshoot software; he also understands how engineering connects to the rest of the business's goals. He knows what needs to happen in the engineering department in order for the company to keep up with the market and grow revenue. He is technical and knows how to build and run development teams. He is married and has young kids, which indicates he is starting to prioritize work-life balance but is still driven to see his team and his company succeed. He has enough experience hiring for different roles that he knows what has worked before and what hasn't. He is a lifetime learner who frequently turns to research, articles and trends to influence how he runs, manages and grows his development team.

RESPONSIBILITIES AND GOALS

Here is where you list what your persona was hired to do and what you most likely would find in their job description. Look at job openings with the vice president of engineering job title on LinkedIn or other job boards for inspiration and ask your sales team to share what their experience has been working with people in these positions. In our example persona, Jonathan is responsible for running the software development team, executing business and technological objectives and strategies and answering to and communicating with the chief technical officer (CTO).

Goals cover what the ideal customer persona wants for their business or team, but you should also think about what they would like for their own careers and life to help you get a more complete picture of them as people. Jonathan would personally like to someday climb the rank to CTO. The more short-term goal for his department, though, would be to build a high-performing software development team who would deliver on schedule and help him show solid growth from quarter to quarter.

PAINS AND FRUSTRATIONS

The last thing you determine when putting together the ideal customer persona is what causes them anxiety and stress. This is information that marketing can use to frame messaging and content to tell a compelling story (because what is a good story without conflict?). Your salespeople will be an invaluable resource to list what these might be. This knowledge will help you center the customer's journey to overcoming their struggles with the help of your product or service.

In our example, the company where Jonathan works is not scaling fast enough internally for them to get everything done on the product road map and meet their delivery schedule. His department is also short-staffed and having a difficult time finding and retaining developers, and he is unsure of how they will achieve road map milestones and delivery schedules. He is getting pulled in numerous directions with supporting past technical initiatives and new projects that seem to keep disrupting the product road map. The team can barely keep on top of their current workload, much less make the additions that upper-level leadership are asking for. As for the vendors he uses, he is unsure of their progress and their technical competency.

The Five-Step Buyer's Journey

Now that you have a clearer image of who your prospective customer is, their responsibilities and the pain and frustrations they face, it's time to imagine their path from their current state, through their process of evaluating your product or service and to their eventual decision to buy.

Journey Step One: The Buyer's Current State

This is where you paint a picture of your ideal customer persona's daily life, before they are aware of your company or the solutions you offer. Starting from this point helps marketing envision how to spot, target and capture the lead's attention to bring them into the funnel.

Jonathan spends 80 percent of his time in meetings. He is the glue between different parts of the organization, drawing the connection between engineering and the business problems the company faces. He meets with the engineering team, management and team leads, as well as the product and marketing and sales teams. His working environment is a hybrid of on-site and remote work, but in both cases the atmosphere is high-pressure and fast-paced. He gets most of his news updates from LinkedIn and a few professional newsletters he subscribes to and reviews during his (very short) breaks.

The rationale for this step is to develop an understanding of the ideal customer persona's current state and what is motivating them to consider your solution.

Journey Step Two: The Buyer's Challenges

Knowing the customer's pain points is essential to determining messaging and course of action. By identifying them, you know how to meet the customer where they are and get that much closer to positioning yourself as their guide to uncovering the solution. Figuring out the following concerns sets the stage for how your solution can help them save themselves from this feared outcome:

- Problems that keep them up at night, including their daily problems and ones that they worry will happen.

- How they fail at their job, including any situations beyond their control that could impact their failure or poor performance.

- What makes their job frustrating or stressful, even when they are not failing. Be sure to include everything that causes them stress, both pressures from the outside and the pressures they put on themselves.

Jonathan has to straddle technical and business concerns, and he worries about capacity-related questions—namely, whether his current team has the bandwidth to complete all their deliverables within the predetermined time frame, if anyone on his team is leaving and how they will find more developers shoulder the workload. In addition to these worries, he must create assurances for the CTO that the product road map is on track and keep his team motivated, learning, succeeding and working together.

Failure points for Jonathan are missed deadlines, incomplete product features and the inability to deliver according to the product road map. These could be results of his own poor decisions or factors that may be out of his control (or some combination of both). Any major staffing decisions he makes is a risk point, and the more difficult it is to find a developer, the higher the stakes.

Journey Step Three: The Buyer's Desired State

Now that you've explored the customer's challenges, it's time to wave the magic wand to discover what the customer's ideal future state would be. Completely remove all barriers of reality and think big! Just remember: whatever their ideal state (their wants), the risks and challenges must be solved first (their needs).

The client's essential needs are non-negotiable for success; they concern the top-of-mind risks that could cause your customer to fail at their job. Next, consider what the client would like to have but are not deal breakers. Both considerations help you conceive of what parts of your offer will benefit your customer (we get deeper into defining your customer's benefits in the next chapter). Remember that success comes from true understanding and building rapport through relevancy and connection. Encouraging this type of thinking in sales and marketing teams elevates performance.

In an ideal world where his wants are fulfilled, Jonathan would have a team full of skilled developers who work well together, are forever-learners, identify problems immediately and collaborate to process challenges and overcome obstacles. They would be innovative, smart, and reliable. However, his non-negotiables are maintaining alignment between his team members, achieving their technological and business goals and delivering on time to the product road map. Missing deadlines, falling behind schedule, incomplete builds and buggy software are not acceptable.

Journey Step Four: The Buyer's Solutions

For your buyer's journey to reach its happily ever after, you need to generate a list of all the possible paths the customer might follow to their ideal resolution—even if that doesn't end with them choosing you.

Your solution is not the only one available, and knowing what options your customer will weigh is vital. They will be using those other options as a measuring stick against yours. However, identifying the competition will also help you determine how and why you provide the one that is most ideal.

For example, Jonathan could solve his capacity problem by choosing to hire more in-house engineers, training up his current team, outsourcing some or all of their software development duties or using off-the-shelf software to integrate into the end solution to save time. And where he gets each of these possible solutions could range as well. For example, he could hire in-house engineers through an internal recruiter or an external staffing company. He could outsource to a domestic resource or to an offshore development company in any number of countries.

Each potential decision a customer considers has advantages and risks, and knowing what those are allows your sales and marketing team to be there as the customer considers both your solution and others. Knowing how you as well as your competitors meet the possible challenges and risks facing the customer creates an advantage for your company. In fact, bringing your competitors' offerings into the conversation can inspire trust and increase your odds of success.

Journey Step Five: The Buyer's Purchase

This is the part of the buyer's journey salespeople risk jumping to before the customer is ready, which typically pushes the lead away and jeopardizes any chance of a sale. **This is so important that we want to state it again: all too often, salespeople see all leads (even the ones who just entered the sales funnel) as ready to buy. Often the lead is simply not at that point in the buyer's journey yet. It's a simple alignment problem, and recognizing this tendency can be a way to create immediate improvement.** After all, how would you feel if you were about to watch a movie and someone walked up and told you the ending before it could even begin?

However, it is helpful for everyone on the integrated sales and marketing team to know from the start how to de-risk choosing to work with your company and what working with you looks like on a practical level. When everyone is aware of those final objections the client may have, the team can collaborate on talking points, blogs, case studies and other content that will be easy to access when those final opportunities to de-risk for the client occur. This consistent awareness will help sales and marketing prepare what they need to bring the buyer's journey to a successful conclusion. Make sure you know:

- How your customer chooses a solution (e.g., who influences their decision, what approval processes they need to go through, whether new teammates who were not present in the early stages of the journey will be making or influencing the decision, etc.)

- Ways that you can make the customer more confident in choosing your solution and therefore de-risk the decision to buy from you (e.g., providing references, case studies, demos, trials, warranties or guarantees)

- Final actions the buyer needs to take to purchase your solution and get started and what may need to happen before the sale can be completed (sometimes the final decision can be delayed by legal processes, the people who need to sign off being unavailable, etc., and it's best to be prepared)

For Jonathan, positive interpersonal experiences help him decide to trust people he works with, as does positive feedback from other teammates involved in evaluating solutions. He wants to be sure that any new developer he adds to the team first asks the right questions to understand the outcomes and end results of the product build before they go into solution mode. On the more practical side, he wants to be able to evaluate a developer's past projects and skills, and he may request a small test project as the final step in evaluating a new addition to the team.

Surveying Your Sales and Marketing Pathway

Knowing who your customers are is a must when it comes to building effective sales strategies, and knowing the road they will travel to ultimately arrive at a purchase is a key component to developing a high-performing sales organization. When you are able to put your company's offerings in the context of your ideal customer's life, you are able to walk with them through each step in their journey and provide them with the information they need to understand the value your solution provides and make a buying decision.

Having all these steps plotted helps you see the big picture: how to get the customer from a lead who doesn't know anything about you and your product to the point of buying. You also grasp all the little choices between those two states, and on that foundation, your sales and marketing team can build a structure to answer each question and provide content that addresses every consideration. This is one of the biggest secrets to highly effective sales and marketing strategies and building a replicable sales generation engine.

Action Items

- Separate your customers into market segments and decide which segments you most want to work with.

- Take note of your customers' job titles and add this as additional categorization related to each of your market segments.

- Determine which market segments you want more of. This is your opportunity to influence how you grow your customer list. We recommend rating your customers according to the criteria you value most.

- Create personas of your ideal customers using the five-step buyer's journey outline. Get specific, so you can actually see who you want to sell to and work to understand what is important to them throughout their journey to a solution to their challenges.

- Fill out each persona's five-step buyer's journey (we have provided a worksheet at the end of this book).

- Bonus: Talk to a sample of the customers who meet your criteria to help validate the work you have done, and then bring it to the market to validate it and learn quickly. Once you see success, you can create repeatable and scalable strategies to move you toward your revenue goals.

Chapter 8:
Features Aren't Benefits, and Benefits Are More Than You Think

Align sales and marketing efforts to what your ideal customers really want from your product or service.

In this chapter, we specify the difference between the features of your product or service and the benefits customers receive. We show why turning benefits into compelling and attractive stories is essential to acquiring the types of customers you want to sell to and why it is vital they be understood across your entire organization.

Again and again, we see companies entrenched in their own narratives— and both sales and marketing departments fall prey to this problem regularly. They are too close to their products and services or too wrapped up in their company's internal drama to understand how their ideal customer might value them. This lack of proper perspective causes sales and marketing departments to lose sight of what would give them an edge over their competitors. They may end up focusing too much on technical details that don't mean much to an interested lead or hyper fixating on one benefit of their product or service without considering whether the lead is looking for that solution.

For example, imagine a software salesperson on a call with a lead. The lead tells the salesperson their company is struggling to find a calendar solution that works for them. By saying this, the lead has presented the salesperson with an enormous opportunity to demonstrate how this product will be of benefit to this specific lead.

Now imagine that instead of taking this opportunity to discuss the benefits of their software's calendar feature, the salesperson skips over the calendar and launches into a spiel about the software's CRM or other features. They do this because they feel it is important to talk about those features or because leads have been interested in learning more about those features in the past. However, in this case, it becomes a missed opportunity.

Making this kind of gaffe is unfortunately common. Many sales and marketing people do not see their offerings through the customer's eyes. The salesperson in our example has fallen prey to their closeness to the product and a specific features-centric script that goes along with it. They have their words mapped out already, and their own agenda takes precedence over the customer's needs. Such a narrow focus often overlooks what problems the customer may be looking to solve with a given product or service.

Overcoming this myopia isn't easy for one salesperson or marketer to do all on their own—they need the help of the team to expand their vision and include the customer's perspective. Until you're able to view the company like an outsider, you miss out on this competitive advantage.

Breaking the barriers between the sales and marketing departments makes room to build a common understanding of your customer's needs. It is also very useful as you go deeper into the benefits found in content that tells a story.

Benefits and Storytelling are Key to Sales and Marketing Integration

If you're in sales or marketing, you might confuse storytelling with content. Content consists of online material such as videos, blogs and social media posts that are meant to educate readers or promote products or services. There's more content out there for leads to sift through than ever before on their social media feeds, in their inboxes and on websites. As they go about their workday and exist in the world, most of what they start to read is quickly abandoned and most of what they do read is completely forgotten.

While a lot of content is simply taking up space, content that abides by the rules of storytelling is much more valuable. People remember stories, and the love of a good story is fundamental to being human. **Your leads can tell the difference between fluff and a narrative relevant to their struggles, conflicts and desires.** This truth must remain at the core of whatever content you create. The secret to writing effectively in a story format is to write about your customers' problems, the advantages they are trying to gain with your solutions and how your product or service can resolve their challenges and provide them with the satisfying resolution they crave.

If you simply dump lists of features onto your website or other forms of marketing content, you are less likely to get positive results. You don't have to guess what your customers want; rather, your sales and marketing team must seek to understand what motivates your leads to interact with your brand. It's easy to get these insights directly from your customers and leads through sales and marketing tools like contact forms, surveys and actual conversations with them. Hearing directly from them helps you identify what your customer needs to gain from using your product or service and what problems you can solve for them. This helps you center their needs and create messaging and content that guides them to your solution.

The Core Factors Inspiring Consumers to Buy

People will always pursue one of two paths when seeking value from your products or services: fear or desire. Either they want to avoid pain or they desire a state of being better than where they are now. All products and services are designed to help the buyer avoid the pain they fear or obtain what they desire. A sales and marketing team's job is to tell a story of how their company's product or service helps the customer along their journey to reach that goal. This is done successfully when the team knows who their customers really are and what benefits a product or service has that solves their unique problem.

Benefits Are Positive Outcomes Resonating with Prospects

If you're still having trouble with the concept of features versus benefits, try replacing the word *benefits* with *positive outcomes*. Consider what positive outcomes the customer will get from the features of your product or service.

Don't stop there. To make a positive outcome, you need to look at the offering and outcome through the lens of your customer.

1. What is the desired state your customer hopes to get when working with you?

2. How does your company get them to a state where their needs are met and their problems are solved?

3. How does each feature of your offering bring them closer to the state that they want?

Let's look at an example of a type of product whose benefits mean different things to different people.

Benefits Are Unique to Each Individual Buyer

One of Tom's clients is a business in the fast-growing protein bar market space. As they researched and learned more about how people buy protein bars, they quickly came to understand people select a protein bar completely based on the perceived benefits of the bar.

A common mistake sales and marketing professionals make is assuming the benefits and features of their products and services apply to all people (or even most people). Ask a few people what they like about their protein bars, and you are very likely to hear a variety of benefits. One person will buy a sugar-free, birthday-cake-flavored bar, while another prefers a dark chocolate–and–cherry vegan bar with sugar. Others want high-energy bars and don't care about the taste. Still others want gluten-free bars.

Trying to make sense of how people select a protein bar through guesswork and brainstorming is not the right approach. The most successful protein bar companies take the time to research and learn why people buy their products. They know how their bar's features translate to benefits for their customers, and they build upon this in their messaging.

What Something Does versus What It Does for the Customer

As a marketer or salesperson, you may be ready to rattle off all the great things about your offering. However, to sell better, you're going to have to face a hard truth—to your prospect, your company is a means to an end; they need a product or service to help them reach their desired state. That's why you must always consider what your features look like in the real world and in what way those features might make a person's life better or easier.

Here are a few examples of how features can be interpreted as benefits for the customer.

Feature (What it is)	Benefit (What it means to the buyer)
Double-wall vacuum insulation	Hot coffee all the way through your morning meeting
100 premier investment funds available	Less stress knowing your retirement will be financially secure; health and longer life
Electricity-powered	Feeling good about yourself by helping the environment and cool because your car is cutting-edge
Five bedrooms	The space for your kids to have their own rooms and stop fighting so much; a peaceful home life
A gym membership	Looking amazing at your daughter's wedding and getting to eat more without guilt
A meal at a restaurant	A luxurious reward after a tough week
A visit to your doctor's or dentist's office	Peace of mind when you get a clean bill of health

You should know why the features of your offering are great, but that doesn't mean your prospects will understand right away. We see many companies fall prey to leading with the left-hand column over the right. Even very large companies who have been around for years fall victim to promoting features over benefits.

What Leading with Benefits Looks Like

Since early 2020, many individuals have not been able or have chosen not to go to the gym due to the COVID-19 pandemic. This means a greater number of people began to purchase exercise equipment for their homes. These buyer's journeys often begin by researching two of the world's most popular fitness equipment companies, NordicTrack and Peloton. Even from their websites, there are noticeable differences in how the two companies present their products and services.

Let's start with Peloton's benefits-focused website strategy. Their flagship product is an exercise bike integrated with a subscription to streamed classes by "celebrity" instructors. Peloton welcomes website visitors by describing how their "game-changing cardio" promises "an immersive cardio experience that will leave you wanting more" and goes on to describe "motivating" instructors, "live weekly classes" that allow users to "feel the energy" and an on-demand library that will let them "find a ride for every mood." These descriptions sound pretty good when you are stuck at home looking to get motivated to exercise.

NordicTrack paints a different picture as they lead with features, rather than benefits. When you visit a sales page for their elliptical, NordicTrack entices you with a five-inch backlit display, 10 percent incline technology, and twenty-two resistance levels. It also brags that "trainers adjust your machine." While these might end up being features users enjoy, reading about it isn't necessarily going to inspire someone off the couch. Their content is focused on features and not benefits.

When Sales and Marketing Gets Too Close to Their Product

NordicTrack has been around since 1975 and is by no means washed up; it was rated in *Consumer Reports'* "Best Buys" in 2016–17 and experienced a surge in sales in 2020. A company like this can afford skillful and experienced sales and marketing teams, but even the highest-caliber sales and marketing teams can lose sight of their benefits.

You might be wondering how it's possible a big company like NordicTrack isn't communicating benefits to their clients. The answer is simple: they're too close to their products. They know the offer too well and have forgotten what these features mean to the average person, who may still not know why those features should matter to them. They see their company from the inside looking out. Peloton sees their company from the outside looking in.

Beef Up Your Benefits-Centered Messaging

You know from the previous chapter that to create a competitive advantage, your company needs a solid, well-articulated identity. By now you'll have answered the question "What do you do?" Now try this one on for size: "What value, benefits, and outcomes does your company provide?" Answering this question sharpens your competitive edge. To make sure you're honing a message correctly, take stock of the type of content you are putting into the world right now as well as the way you're speaking to leads about your offerings. The value this content brings lies in the core benefits you provide to customers. Those core benefits are also what define your leadership in the market.

Communicating Benefits with Your Marketing Copy

When attempting to talk about benefits, many company websites and printed materials start every sentence with the words *we* or *our*:

- Our people are our competitive advantage!

- Our team brings 150 years of collective experience!

- Our mission is to provide exemplary support to our valued customers!

- We believe in customer service—we do the hard work, so our clients don't have to!

- We are committed to our clients!

To be blunt, these qualities are the bare minimum of what people expect from you, and your competitors can all make these claims. A commitment to working hard, providing exemplary customer service and support and hiring the best of the best aren't differentiators—they're the price of entry in most industries. Fail to pay the price of entry, and a business likely won't stand a chance. In fact, shouting these qualities from the home page might make website visitors raise an eyebrow.

People don't hire or buy from your company because you have the tools and technologies you need to run your business and achieve your revenue goals. They hire or buy from your company because of the benefits you offer and their faith that you can deliver those benefits.

Your entire website, including the About page, shouldn't simply underscore why your company is so fantastic. Instead, your website should speak to and serve the needs of your target audience. Your customers keep you in business, and your prospects keep that business flowing, so tailor your site to their needs, their questions, their priorities and their desired outcomes. Don't tell prospects that you're great. Show them what you've done to make your customers' lives better and how you might do the same for them.

Selling with Conversations Based on Positive Outcomes or Benefits

You might recall Realtor Sales Skills, Karl's client who focuses on selling educational programs on real estate sales and marketing. We received a very telling insight when observing how two of their key salespeople talk to prospective customers.

Salesperson One talks to prospects about what the program does, how it works and what it costs. He sells features, citing facts and figures and noting that the program takes six weeks to complete and includes twelve modules.

Salesperson Two talks to prospects about why they're thinking about starting the program. Many prospects tell her they're frustrated with their current job. *What's so frustrating about your job?* she asks them. Many of them say their job limits their free time. *What would you do if you had more free time?* They would relax more often. They would spend more time with their family. They would exercise daily. They would travel more frequently.

She listens to what these prospects say and processes what they tell her. Once she knows what they're after, she tailors the discussion, explaining that the program will provide an income stream that enables them to live and travel where they want, when they want. They can even pick their own work hours, giving them the employment flexibility they're seeking. Once she has their undivided attention, she does a deeper dive, explaining how the program works.

You probably won't be surprised to hear that Salesperson Two closes 50 percent more business than Salesperson One.

Whether you are writing marketing copy or having a conversation with a lead, you need to know the real benefits of what you're selling. The best way to really confirm what those are is by speaking with your customers and asking them through a survey, face-to-face or on the phone what they're looking for when they seek you out. Then, take that information and use it to shape the way you communicate about your products.

Action Items

- Read *Building a StoryBrand* by Donald Miller to learn more about how to center your customer as the hero and truly take them on a journey.

- Use questionnaires, surveys and discussions with your salespeople to define what your customers view as benefits and what they are looking to gain from your product or service. Ask your customers and prospects what future state they're looking to achieve with your offering or in a similar offering. You might be surprised how many salespeople and marketers don't do this!

- Look at your current offerings and write out their features. Now, consider what each feature's outcome would be if used in the real world. Then, take the next step and identify how each outcome could be seen as a benefit and who might see it that way.

- Agree on the three-to-five most important benefits of your company's products or services across multiple market segments. Feature these on your website home page.

Part Two:

The Right Processes for Sales and Marketing Integration

Chapter 9:
The Integrated Sales and Marketing Funnel

Align your sales and marketing team to organize leads, get higher-quality leads and improve sales performance.

In this chapter, we review how to break down silos to create an integrated sales funnel, map the buyer's journey to the funnel and get ideas for activities to perform within each stage, as well as how to assign roles and responsibilities.

In the past, marketing teams threw out a wide net, using a variety of advertising approaches and just hoping something would catch. These efforts were not always aligned with the sales team and often alienated the customer-facing work of sales. Today, it is possible to link marketing activities to sales activities to create a seamless buyer's journey, an end-to-end sales process that maximizes marketing and sales effectiveness. In this chapter, we review the stages of the sales funnel in more detail, talk about how it organizes leads and describe activities sales and marketing can use in tandem to close sales.

The Fundamentals of the Integrated Sales and Marketing Funnel

The sales funnel organizes leads in order of how close they are to making a purchase. By doing so, you can develop strategies and tactics that align with each of these three populations and that move leads from one grouping to the next until those leads make a purchase.

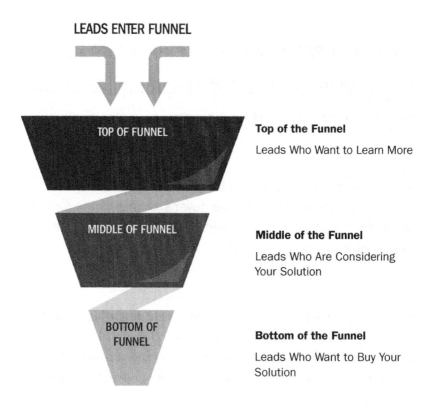

LEADS ENTER FUNNEL

TOP OF FUNNEL

MIDDLE OF FUNNEL

BOTTOM OF FUNNEL

Top of the Funnel

Leads Who Want to Learn More

Middle of the Funnel

Leads Who Are Considering Your Solution

Bottom of the Funnel

Leads Who Want to Buy Your Solution

While leads can enter the funnel at any stage, a typical buyer's journey starts at the top of the funnel, moves to the middle of the funnel and ends at the bottom of the funnel. Following is a rundown of what happens in these stages and examples of activities that leverage the strengths of sales and marketing in each.

Top of the Funnel—Leads Who Want to Learn More

Leads who enter here include people who have made initial contact with your company via marketing outreach. Maybe they have signed up for your newsletter, downloaded a marketing magnet, followed your company on social media, scanned their badge at your tradeshow booth, connected with a member of your team at a networking event or met you through a strategic partner. Many marketers call these marketing qualified leads (MQLs).

These leads aren't ready to buy. They've dipped their toes into the water and are still deciding whether they want to jump in. Far too often these leads are sent directly to the sales team. When the sales team reaches out, misalignment often drives those leads away. Don't work hard to sell leads who are not ready to buy! Rather, work on moving them to the next stage in the funnel.

What Leads Want: At this stage, leads are looking to learn more about your company and how your company understands their challenges and problems. They want to know that investing more time in learning about your offerings is a smart choice.

Lead Ownership: The marketing team owns top-of-funnel messaging and resources. Marketing can develop content that tells your story and aligns with each type of lead entering your funnel. Their research and the data they collect should always be shared with sales to help them anticipate what content leads are looking at the most.

Activities: Top-of-funnel strategies and tactics should meet leads where they are to offer useful information. This high-value, low-pressure stage of the sales funnel positions your company as an information resource and moves leads further down your funnel. Activities should require low or no commitment and not push leads to purchase.

SAMPLE TOP-OF-FUNNEL ACTIVITIES

Newsletters: Include information leads need to know about their situation, the benefits that come from your product or service and how your company solves their challenges and problems.

Social Media Posts: Provide a consistent stream of relevant top-of-funnel content in all your social channels.

Marketing Email Sequences: Build automated email sequences, giving leads educational content to move them from the top of the funnel to the middle of the funnel and create data points to measure each lead's level of interest.

Invitations: Invite top-of-funnel leads to events where they can learn more about your company and your offerings. Examples include on-demand videos and invitations to webinars, panel discussions, demonstrations and workshops.

Thought Leadership: Engage top-of-funnel leads by developing educational content that creates aha moments and provides useful information to make their lives better. Thought leadership content can be incorporated into any of these activities.

Middle of the Funnel—Leads Who Are Considering Your Solution

The middle of the funnel is a transition point where leads consider moving forward with a solution to their problems. They have reached this point by interacting with content that moves from educating them about you and your company to digging deeper into the benefits of your specific solutions. Sales and marketing professionals often call these sales qualified leads (SQLs). They're becoming interested enough in your company to consider your solution as an option.

As with the other stages of the sales funnel, the middle of the funnel has levels or gradations of leads. Some leads will be only slightly interested in your solution, while others will be very interested. It's in this stage that the sales department is introduced to these leads.

What Leads Want: At this stage, leads are looking to learn more about your solutions and the outcomes they create. They want to solve a problem or improve the quality of their lives. Leads in the funnel may end up deciding the timing isn't right or their problems aren't big enough to warrant further investigation. They'll also begin evaluating all available options to solve their problems, including solutions offered by your competitors.

Lead Ownership: Leads at this stage have taken some type of action to show they want to learn more about your solutions. Your sales team's job is to create revenue by engaging people who are considering your solutions. The marketing team's job is to create relevant resources and provide middle-of-funnel support to turn leads into SQLs, ones primed for sales conversations.

Activities: The strategies and tactics you want to deploy in the middle of the funnel should support leads in their evaluation of your solutions and the outcomes they create. We recommend creating high-value resources that are quick to digest and easy to understand. Share these resources on multiple platforms and channels so leads can learn the way they want to learn. Possibilities include sections of your newsletter dedicated to your solutions, middle-of-funnel social media content and opportunities for group or individual learning like live webinars, informational presentations and Q&A sessions with a panel of experts.

This is the time for sales to start reaching out to leads; marketing materials can start extending invitations for leads to interact with your salespeople. Sales outreach can be more direct than in the top of the funnel, and this is the point where sales should be especially aware of what the marketing team is doing and where they might step in with one-on-one follow-ups either via personalized emails or even phone calls.

SAMPLE MIDDLE-OF-FUNNEL ACTIVITIES

Presentations and Webinars: Providing middle-of-funnel leads with educational opportunities and ways they can experience your solutions will move these leads to the bottom of the funnel. Examples include on-demand videos, webinars, panel discussions, group presentations, demonstrations and workshops.

Appointments: After every presentation, include a next step that invites leads to learn more (usually a one-on-one appointment with the sales team) and move closer to a purchase.

Post-Presentation Outreach: Not everyone who attends a presentation will schedule an appointment, but that doesn't mean that they're not interested in learning more or making a purchase. Post-presentation outreach in the form of emails, texts and phone calls is essential. **Sometimes all leads need is a nudge from a professional salesperson to keep them moving through the sales funnel toward a purchase.**

Data-Driven Outreach: One of the best things about digital marketing is the ability to track activities such as email opens and clicks at a group and individual level. The resulting performance data can provide a list of middle-of-funnel leads who have shown interest through their digital actions. Your sales team can use this data to activate different kinds of sales outreach, such as emails, texts, phone calls and voice mails.

Sales Email Sequences: Sales email sequences focus on your solutions, outcomes and examples of their success. Sales email sequences can move middle-of-funnel leads to the bottom of the funnel.

Bottom of the Funnel—Leads Who Want to Buy Your Solution

The bottom of the funnel is where leads are strongly considering purchasing your solution. While some bottom-of-funnel leads are more ready to buy than others, all of these leads have moved from the consideration stage to the purchase stage. Some call these leads opportunities.

What Leads Want: At this stage, leads have moved toward a state where they want to de-risk their decision and understand your value and the outcomes your solution creates. Yours may be the only solution leads are considering or one of many. Your sales team will want to proactively address any concerns or objections. This is the stage where your success can compound as your sales team gets better and better at increasing leads' confidence that your solution will create the outcomes they really want.

Lead Ownership: Guiding leads toward a purchase is where most salespeople excel. Here, you are way beyond providing resources and making the case for your company. Leads will either buy quickly or need support in making the best decision. The more your sales team understands the characteristics of bottom-of-funnel leads, the more sales they'll close.

Activities: The bottom-of-funnel strategies and tactics you architect need to address the leads' purchasing process. Your sales team will need to customize their actions with bottom-of-funnel leads to fit each unique buying situation.

Focus on what your sales team can do to continue to build momentum toward the sale and navigate any roadblocks that get in the way of a purchase. This is the stage where sales skills really pay off, and the effects of all the priming marketing has done to get these leads where they are will support the sales team's work. Leads want to do everything they can to ensure they're making the right decision; they don't want to make a costly mistake or buy the wrong solution. Instead, they want to feel confident about the value they'll receive if they make the purchase. The more information available to them, even at this last stage in the funnel, the better.

The strategies and tactics used at this stage need to be carefully designed to give each lead exactly what they need to move forward with their decision to buy. Building an inventory of resources and training your team to use them will enable your team to perform at a high level. One thing that Karl has found to be helpful for sales to do is keep a running list of FAQs—questions that leads frequently ask or misunderstandings they often see when they reach this stage of the funnel. Additionally, a document detailing why or why not leads chose to buy is invaluable for both sales and marketing to improve talking points and content. These can be shared among the sales team, and they can also be passed to marketing to inform middle-of-funnel content more strongly.

SAMPLE BOTTOM-OF-FUNNEL ACTIVITIES

Case Studies or Success Stories: These resources increase lead confidence by painting a picture of a common problem and how your solution created a satisfying outcome.

Ambassadors or Reference Accounts: Leads close to buying often want one final confidence check before making a purchase. They may want to have a candid conversation with a current customer who has purchased your solution. You can have pre-screened customer ambassadors at the ready or reference accounts who may agree to talk to your leads about their experience working with you. While both strategies can be effective, ensure that the ambassador or reference account is happy with your company and up-to-date on your offerings.

Guarantees: Having some form of guarantee directly reduces a buyer's risk and increases their confidence. Guarantees can be structured in many ways but typically provide money back, additional services or time to create a specific outcome or some other way to ensure the solution is successful. The clearer and simpler a guarantee, the better this strategy is at moving sales forward.

Samples, Test Drives and Trial Periods: This strategy is all about letting leads experience the solution you provide at no risk or cost. These highly effective strategies require intentional design as to how they work, how they are managed and how the sales team uses them to increase close rates. Samples, test drives and trial periods alone aren't strong enough to close sales at consistent rates; instead, collaboration from the sales team, support team and delivery team is needed to guide leads to a purchase.

Ride Along: This strategy lets leads experience your solution firsthand, allowing them to understand the results of your offering through a demo or the eyes of a current customer.

Strategy, Processes and People Lead to Sales Funnel Success

Understanding the different stages of the sales funnel, what motivates a lead who inhabits that stage and what types of activities are effective will help put your team into action. Sales and marketing will begin to form strategies based on the flow of leads from top to bottom, assigning appropriate roles and responsibilities as they select activities to include in the sales and marketing process.

We will go into more detail about how to optimize the handoff from marketing to sales in the middle of the funnel, as well as how to measure success of each sales and marketing activity, in later chapters. The key is to supercharge the funnel by having sales and marketing teams coordinate their efforts and work together to build activity in the funnel.

Action Items

- Ask marketing to review current data to see what content and topics leads are most interested in, including most-visited web pages, most-clicked newsletters and social media posts with the highest engagement. Consider this data regarding how your current sales processes and activities apply to the different stages of the sales funnel.

- Have the marketing team send a survey to your prospect database telling them that you're hard at work crafting a new video series, e-book, etc., and want to see if they have any particular topics they would like you to cover. This not only gives you more insight into what topics your audience is interested in but can also reveal new areas of interest that aren't yet on your radar.

- Appoint a marketing liaison who shares what marketing initiatives are in the works so they're aware of what's coming and the content and messaging that leads receive. That way, salespeople know how leads have been educated about the company and how they can use your products or services in their jobs, and they can also give input based on what questions and concerns they are receiving from leads.

- Appoint someone from the sales team to be a point of contact for marketing activities and have them regularly attend webinars, review new content and keep the rest of the sales team up-to-date. Every person at your company should receive your newsletter and follow your social media accounts, and someone from sales should be tasked with more carefully monitoring this content.

- Develop a shared document of frequently asked questions sales receive from leads, as well as a document detailing feedback on why or why not leads chose to buy the company's solution. This content from sales can inform future content and campaigns marketing spearheads.

- Foster an attitude of gratitude between teams! Encourage the sales team to share wins and thank marketing for their work to qualify leads and share data, and marketing to thank sales for sharing their firsthand experiences with leads and customers.

Chapter 10:
Fixing Your Lead Problem as an Integrated Team

Solve lead generation problems and nurture those leads in the sales funnel.

In this chapter, we correct misconceptions that sales and marketing teams have about leads and demonstrate how working your integrated funnel improves lead quality and conversion rates.

Not closing enough sales to meet your revenue targets can be frustrating, confusing, disappointing and dangerous for the survival of your business. Understanding the sales funnel, defining the different activities that take place in each stage and knowing each person's role in it are keys to demystifying why you aren't hitting your sales goals. These insights offer a doorway to discovering where exactly your lead problems lie and why leads are getting stuck in the funnel. It also provides the clues to how sales and marketing teams can work together to unstick them.

In this chapter, we share guidance for how marketing and sales can work together to identify high-value leads and create more impactful strategies that move warm leads further down the sales funnel. We also show you how to identify leads who may waste resources that could instead be devoted to people more likely to purchase from you. Let's start with an example of how sales and marketing teams collaborated to improve marketing content using a webinar strategy to generate appointments for the sales team.

Enhancing Content to Generate Higher-Quality Appointments

Once the sales and marketing teams at our sample company Realtor Sales Skills had defined the ownership for each stage of their sales funnel, they began to explore where leads were getting stuck. The two teams started collaborating more frequently to solve these issues and grow sales. They did this by looking at quantitative data from their CRM, reviewing chat threads from past webinars and asking the sales team to share the most common feedback and questions they received from leads who recently attended a webinar.

For Realtor Sales Skills, webinars were a major sales appointment driver, and they became a quintessential team effort. Marketing would attract people to the webinars from several sources, including Facebook ads, email sequences and social shares, and those leads were put into the CRM. During the webinar, the sales team would interact with attendees using the chat function. The sales team would then schedule appointments with leads during or immediately following the webinars.

The webinars were excellent at painting a vision of what the training programs could do for realtors. They explained how these programs could improve realtors' lives and how a realtor could experience significant growth in their business and increase their income. Still, a problem emerged from this approach. Even though the webinars were lengthy and inspirational, the details of the program were covered at a very surface level. While the webinars certainly generated appointments and excitement, they fell short for some of the attendees who wanted to understand more about the program before spending time with a salesperson.

This all came to surface when the marketing team started to look at all the clues in front of them. In reviewing the past three months of webinar chats, they found a common theme. The chat was filled with the same questions over and over: How does the program work? When will you cover the details of the program in the webinar? How much does the program cost? When will you demo the platform or review the details of the program?

These questions showed up in the feedback from the sales team too. Each salesperson had numerous stories of attendees showing up to their appointments with similar questions, and the most consistent feedback coming from the leads was the need for more specifics about the actual training program. Many leads stated that they thought about not showing up for their appointment because they didn't have enough information to determine whether the program would be valuable to them. After looking at the quantitative data, the team observed appointments booked from the webinar had a 15 percent higher non-attendance rate than appointments from other sources.

The sales and marketing team realized the Realtor Sales Skills webinars were great at highlighting benefits and outcomes of the program, but they hadn't balanced this with practical information about how the product worked. It was not until sales and marketing took proactive steps to come together as a team, get into conversation, support one another and share observations and data that they realized they could improve their sales performance.

Your Pillars of Thought Leadership

We call the areas where your company stands out and provides unique value to your customers your pillars of thought leadership. Maybe one is the quality of the products; another could be how knowledgeable your team is or how responsive to customer inquiries the team members are. These differentiating qualities are your pillars of thought leadership, and they present benefits to the customer and are vital in structuring your content and voice. Each team member knowing what they are and how to communicate them serves as a compass to navigate through problems you may have with leads at different stages of the funnel, particularly when you need to create content that is engaging and informative.

When people research your company, they want to know if you have what it takes to solve their problems. To get started, ask yourself the following questions:

- What does our company do better than anyone else's company?

- How is our company different from other companies like ours?

Remember, to really be sure the pillars are things that you do well and are appreciated for, you need to verify those facts with your customers. That means it's once again time to use your secret weapon: sales and marketing alignment. Different members of each team have insights on what your customers like from various perspectives. Marketing can contribute data from Google Analytics and Google Search Console to see which pages are the most popular on your website and which blogs get the most traffic. Your sales team can provide ideas based on their conversations with prospective customers. By the time prospects reach the marketing team, they have often done a lot of research already.

Once you have done your research, come up with at least three pillars of thought leadership of your own and get ready to use them in your content and campaign. We talk more about the kinds of collaborative content your team can create and automate, as well as how to measure its effectiveness, in chapter thirteen. Being aligned on your pillars of thought leadership helps you build content that draws appropriate leads into your funnel and serves them at every step in their buyer's journey.

Too Few Leads: Lack of Relevant Content

One of the most common complaints we hear from our sales and marketing clients is they want more leads to hit their targets. Often, the blame is put on marketing, with the common rallying cry being "We need more leads!" Management, in turn, often identifies the problem as a top-of-funnel problem and puts the responsibility to ramp up lead generation on the marketing team. However, the solution is always more complicated.

A comprehensive approach to sales and marketing integration is vital to fueling a sustainable and scalable lead-generating engine, not only for lead quantity but also for lead quality. Top-of-funnel lead generation activities require cooperation between teams. An excellent example is digital content.

Digital content is the primary driver to bring leads into the top of the funnel. **Far too often the marketing team writes websites and other digital content with no input from the sales team.** This is a critical missed opportunity to improve the effectiveness of the top of the funnel and attract the attention of qualified prospects. Sales and marketing teams must work together to create valuable, relevant content if they want to have breakthrough performance. Here are some ways sales and marketing teams can make sure they are using all tools at their disposal to write relevant content:

- Keep a list of key phrases and topics the sales team sees and hears from the leads they interact with; then use this as data to shape digital content strategy.

- Understand what the top-of-funnel content leads want and use Google and social media ad buys to put your related content in front of these audiences.

- If there are higher demand periods or seasonality in your business, recognize them and develop campaigns or content calendars that ramp up during those windows.

- Develop lists of blog topics by bringing your sales and marketing teams together to collaborate and leave the meetings with agreement on prioritized blog topics, owners and timing (schedules). Conduct keyword research around the proposed blog topics to see which exact phrases are being searched the most by your audience on Google.

- Write relevant, thought-leadership content that will be shared by influencers and referral sources to expand your reach. Build a list of strategic (but not competitive) partners who also produce great content, have an active presence on social media and possess an engaged email list. When you write your blog article, make sure you hyperlink it to several relevant articles written by these partners. Personally let them know you linked to their content and ask them if they'd be open to sharing your blog with their audience.

- Remember that stories are a very effective way to communicate with your audiences and are more easily shared and remembered than facts and figures. Develop story-based content that can be used in your digital content strategies.

- Review your past social posts that had the most interactions and develop similar social posts in the future to extend your reach and effectiveness. You can also repurpose content and use the same exact posts that were the best performers from the previous quarter.

- Have the sales team take note of the most interesting sales conversions they have during the week and watch for trends and common threads of interest. This makes for great top-of-funnel content.

No matter what marketing strategies you implement to generate more leads, the effectiveness of each strategy will be dramatically improved if the content aligns to each target audience you want to reach and meets them where they are in their own unique buyer's journey. This is best achieved through collaboration between sales and marketing teams and an intentional mapping of content to these different journeys. If you are developing content and ads to get that content in front of a specific audience, make sure the messaging and images align to that audience. It's going to take the collaboration of an integrated marketing and sales team to get this right. The result will be a solid content strategy to bring more and better-qualified leads into your sales funnel.

Too Many Leads: Quantity versus Quality

Believe it or not, too many leads can cause real problems for a sales team as well. Sales and marketing professionals easily fall into a common pattern of thinking that causes inefficient use of funds— thinking that sheer number of leads is the most important part of lead generation. **In fact, focusing on quantity of leads over quality wastes money and time, when just a little more information at the top of the funnel could bring in leads much more suited for your offerings.**

When Realtor Sales Skills ramped up a new campaign to bring in more appointments for the sales team, the initial numbers were off the charts. From the outside, the campaign looked like a win since the number of appointments had doubled in volume. However, when the team looked closer, they found a significant number of appointments were booked by leads who didn't live within North America. These leads were close but unusable based on the content of Realtor Sales Skills' courses. Instead of this campaign being a roaring success, it was an expensive tactic that took up the sales team's time with leads they couldn't close. There were now over one hundred unqualified leads receiving marketing automations, newsletters and retargeted ads with a CTA to book an appointment with a salesperson. This was a frustrating waste of time for the sales team.

Another example is a company who offers chartered flights starting at $5,000. When they began to run paid ads, the leads started rolling in. However, as soon as the lead got on a call with a salesperson, they discovered how much the flights cost. At that point, a large percentage of leads would realize they could not afford the company's services. That pricing detail hadn't been included on the original paid ads or on the landing page. Despite the number of leads the ad brought in, the quality of those leads was diluted because of the vagueness of the ads that hooked them in the first place. If the company had included a starting price, there would have been fewer leads clicking on the ad, but those leads would be much more likely to continue with the process of buying. As it was, the company was wasting money on ads that attracted leads who were not right for the service being offered.

Contacting the wrong leads can waste the sales team's time, and a tidal wave of unsuitable leads can be just as harmful to your bottom line as a trickle of qualified ones. Better communication between teams, focusing on clear and direct content along with mid-funnel activities and nurturing will help improve lead quality and cut down on wasted time. If your diligence and collaboration results in leads qualifying themselves out of the funnel, that's fine. By using clear and direct content on your website, people are more likely to understand whether they are a good fit for your products or services. Sales and marketing alignment on ideal customer personas and what qualifies a lead helps solve this problem. It also helps you develop stronger content once your more-qualified leads travel lower in the funnel.

Using Middle-of-Funnel Content to Move Leads from Marketing to Sales

The middle of the funnel is key to moving MQLs to SQLs, then driving them toward a closed sale. While the top of the funnel belongs mostly to marketing and the bottom mostly to sales, the middle can seem like a no-man's-land. If the team isn't careful, the responsibilities inside of this stage can be murky, and leads can get stuck when sales and marketing teams are unsure of who is responsible for what. However, with careful planning and clear assignments of different team members to different tasks, sales and marketing teams can collaborate on middle-of-funnel content, automation and outreach tactics to drive sales growth. This collaboration can help create:

- Focused website landing pages that express the benefits your ideal customer prioritizes and whose missions match up with the content of whatever ad or post brought them to that page

- High-quality downloadable content such as e-books, webinars, product demos, online events, white papers, technical specs, slide decks and other content created specifically for your ideal customer personas and the unique journeys they will take

- Email marketing content that educates your customer and drives quality lead cultivation, educating leads so they can make informed decisions about whether to move closer to buying your solution

- Improved CTAs that inspire leads to engage with the content they get from you, further qualifying them to move from marketing activities to interacting with the sales team

Marketers are responsible for creating great content and automations, and salespeople can provide insights as to how leads decide whether to buy. With those insights, marketers can then use their skills to communicate the benefits leads are seeking from the first moment a prospect makes contact via a social post, ad or website landing page. We introduce specific ways to build these digital marketing content touchpoints and automations together, using your sales funnel as a guide, in chapters twelve and thirteen. You will also learn how to score leads to determine how they are progressing through the middle of the funnel and evaluate how your strategies and processes are working and not working.

Not All Leads Are Created Equal

When salespeople treat every lead the same way, they're putting your organization's sales investment and performance at serious risk. They're diminishing the ROI of every dollar spent on marketing to bring in leads. They're also alienating many of those leads, inadvertently pushing them into your competitors' camps. When salespeople treat all leads the same, they can't sell to their full potential.

Think about your own shopping experiences. Most everyone has casually strolled into a clothing store that was advertising to their demographic. Often a salesperson approaches who asks, "Can I help you find something?"

In response, you may have said, "I'm just looking," which means, "Please leave me alone. I'm just browsing, and I'm not ready to buy just yet."

Now, think about if that salesperson said, "I'm going to grab some clothes that I think you'll like and set up a dressing room for you." Worse, what if the salesperson went on to say, "Can I ask how much you're looking to spend?"

You probably would feel uncomfortable. You may even leave the store and never return.

In this example, marketing drew you into the store, but you weren't ready to buy. In the same way, many leads visit your site or join your mailing list because they just want to browse. They're interested in learning more, but they're not ready to talk about making a purchase.

If you treat every lead as if they're ready to buy, you'll scare many of them away. For this reason, you need to understand all the different types of leads that marketing sends your way. You also need to develop strategies and related tactics to meet these leads where they are in their journey and effectively guide them to the next stage of their decision-making process.

A Tale of Two Leads

To demonstrate how sales and marketing integration enables sales-people to successfully guide leads toward becoming customers, let's consider the journeys of two leads.

Both leads register to attend a live webinar to learn about a B2B offering. At the end of the webinar, their CTA is to schedule an appointment with a salesperson. Both leads attend the webinar and stick around until the end. Afterward, Lead One schedules a call with a salesperson, and Lead Two does not.

What should your sales team do next? Should they reach out to both leads or only Lead One? When should outreach begin? Should email outreach precede any calls? Should marketing send out a series of automated follow-up emails on behalf of the sales team? It can be tempting to jump into action, but before the sales team starts calling and emailing, let's consider where the leads are in their own respective journeys.

First, consider why your leads may have signed up for the webinar in the first place and what they want to walk away with. Usually, people register for a webinar because they want to learn more about the problems or challenges they're facing and understand how your company solves those problems. They may have some curiosity about your specific solution, but it's more likely they are seeking knowledge. What they don't want is a sales pitch.

The people who attend your webinar won't all have the same experience, nor will they all take the same next step. Some leads may leave the webinar early. They may not believe the information is relevant to them or may have other time commitments. Some may stay for the entire presentation but won't be ready to move forward. Some may be inspired to make a purchase right away.

Lead One scheduled a call with your sales team. If the call is that day, the salesperson should review information in the CRM, including when the lead first opted in to learn about your company, how many emails they've received and what content or lead magnets they've opened or downloaded. Your salesperson should also do some Google and LinkedIn research ahead of the call to get background knowledge on the lead and their company.

If the sales appointment is one or more days in the future, your salesperson should also prime the lead with an email to introduce themselves. They may share additional resources the salesperson thinks relevant to the lead's solution. It is also a good idea to prepare the lead for the call. The sales rep can ask if they have any questions or if they would like to cover any specific information. That way, the salesperson themselves can prepare, helping to move the lead further through the sales funnel.

The reason Lead Two stayed for the entire webinar but didn't book an appointment with your sales team isn't clear. Chances are there was something the lead wanted to learn from the webinar but did not get. Finding out the reason for this behavior is necessary for getting the lead unstuck, so you can improve your process and give them the information they need or lower the risk of taking the next step.

This is where the sales team can come to the rescue. Having your salespeople reach out in the right way will help solve this problem and get answers. They can ask for feedback or if they have questions. This knowledge puts the sales and marketing team in the position to know what to do next to move the lead closer to a purchase. In many cases, being attentive to the lead nudges them closer to the bottom of the funnel.

Solving Your Lead Problem by the Numbers

Sometimes increasing sales looks like a simple math problem. The logic we often see from our clients goes something like this: *we close*

25 percent of our leads; therefore, if we can double the number of leads, we can double our closed sales. Seems logical, right? However, simply getting more leads does not guarantee a proportionate number of closed sales.

For example, a company who closes 80 percent of their leads from referrals is not usually closing 80 percent of all leads in the funnel. Referrals have a much higher probability of turning into new business than typical top-of-funnel leads generated by marketing. Referrals generally enter the sales funnel at the bottom, and most marketing-generated leads who are unaware of the brand enter the top of the funnel. In the case of referrals, the customer providing the referral did most of the marketing work, and the lead is entering your funnel with a high probability of buying.

If the business described here is currently fed solely by referrals, bringing in other types of leads will lower their close rate. It will not stay at 80 percent if all leads in the funnel are included. Moving leads from the top to the bottom of the funnel means they need a significantly larger number of marketing generated leads to ultimately create a sale.

Top-of-Funnel Lead Math with Google Ads

Google Ads are an excellent source of top-of-funnel activity. They help build your online brand and also drive inquiries. However, be careful of using Google Ads only to generate leads. This can result in many un-qualified leads and a higher ad spend. Often when generating leads from Google Ads, when the goal is to simply get more leads, the percentage of qualified leads begins to decrease as the number of leads increases.

Imagine a Google Ad campaign to generate leads reaching two thousand people per month. If the campaign does fairly well, about 5 percent of the searchers will click on your ads. In this scenario, one hundred people will visit your website landing page. If 10 percent of those people complete a contact form or connect your sales team, you are left with ten MQLs. If 10 percent of those people buy, the result is one sale.

Let's say you target higher-converting keywords but reach only one thousand people per month. If the click-through rate increases to 10 percent due to these targeted search terms, then you still get one hundred leads per month—however, the quality of the leads will increase, and the spend on Google Ads will generally decrease. A 10 percent close rate will still result in one sale, but it will come with less time needed from the sales team and a lower ad spend.

There are a couple of things you can do to get more sales with this strategy. One, you can increase the number of targeted keyword search terms and spend more money to have your ad served to more people. Two, you can equip your sales team to support them closing at a higher rate than 10 percent. In this example, let's assume the strategies will either increase leads or increase sales; as soon as any of the conversion metrics decrease, you will need more leads to generate the same sales outcomes. This creates a scenario where the number of leads needed to create a sale continues to shift (typically downward) and sales forecasting becomes more and more variable and uncertain.

The lesson here is lead volume alone doesn't necessarily equate to increased revenue. If you want to develop an efficient sales engine with a degree of predictability and generally forecastable ROI, you must know the number of qualified leads required to achieve your sales targets.

Sales and marketing alignment can help you reach more qualified leads without just throwing more money at the problem. Your sales and marketing teams can collaborate to figure out ways to optimize the qualified leads coming into the funnel. One example is coming together to optimize the search terms you use in your ads. Interviewing salespeople about the major questions, concerns and benefits your real-life customers are looking for can inspire the marketing team's search for good keywords. After getting input from sales and doing research of their own, the people who click on your ads may be more likely to buy once they do get to your website.

By taking into consideration the ideal customer personas you've built, their buyer's journeys and how your sales and marketing funnels maps that journey, you can begin to address where your lead problem lies. Review your sales and marketing content and practices together through the lens of the leads you want to generate and nurture. From there, you can start adapting content and processes that meet them where they are in their Google research.

Action Items

- Bring sales and marketing teams together to select and determine content topics and opportunities in the sales funnel to move prospects along their buyer's journey. As you do this, review your current website to see whether there is content associated with each stage of the funnel. Additionally, evaluate whether your content is well-written and clearly communicates the value your solution provides to the customer.

- Focus on content topics your prospects and customers desire, informed by your sales team's real-life customer interactions. These topics are about the key benefits they want and also help them evaluate solutions based on where they are in the funnel and their buying journey. Once you have done that, you can create top-of-funnel content that addresses the priorities of your ideal customers and attracts people to your brand as well as middle-of-funnel content that moves leads from one stage of the funnel to the next.

- Review the CTAs you include in your current content. Are they all asking the lead to make a purchase, or are some sharing access to more information and resources like newsletters, white papers and webinars? Evaluate how they meet the needs of the ideal customer personas you generated (explained in chapter seven) and how you expect they will move leads through the middle of the integrated sales and marketing funnel.

- Evaluate where most of your paying customers have come from to reach the point of buying from you. Determine how much money you spend on generating leads through each channel and whether they are resulting in enough sales to justify the expense. Bring your team together to discuss how you might optimize these top-of-funnel lead-generation tactics.

Chapter 11:
Sales and Marketing Alignment Fuels a Winning Sales Strategy

Build accountability to each part of the sales funnel with an integrated sales and marketing team.

In this chapter, we talk about how team members can map their responsibilities to different stages of the sales funnel and how both sales and marketing can value one another's feedback and contributions to grow sales.

Consider a meeting we had with the VP of sales, CFO, CEO and brand-new CMO at a SaaS company, Property Management Analytics. From the beginning, the conversation was focused on the sales and marketing funnel and marketing's accountability for moving leads into and through the funnel to get them ready for sales. The CFO started the discussion because they needed a stronger understanding of the sales forecasts to manage the financial needs of the company.

"I don't really like the idea of the sales funnel," the CMO responded. "I want to look at marketing as contributing to the overall sales growth of the company, not just a part of it. I see my role as the leader managing the brand, and anything related to a 'sales funnel' is outside of my responsibilities."

As we dug deeper, we learned the CMO saw marketing's role as promoting the value the company offered and what benefits the offerings would bring customers, then crafting language that fit the brand's personality. Therefore, he expected marketing tasks to float on the surface of the funnel as they invited leads in through an omni-channel approach. What he didn't realize was this lack of integration and depth of involvement in the funnel meant projecting revenue wouldn't be easy.

The CFO and CEO were asking for concrete projections: How many people did marketing expect to bring into the funnel based on each of their activities from Facebook and Google Ads to webinars and other gated content? What budget would marketing need to generate these leads, and ultimately, what would the ROI of that spend be? They wanted to understand how their investments would pay off in sales revenues. They wanted to quantify what would bring a certain number of people into the funnel and then apply this number to the company's baseline close rate so they could forecast revenue.

As the meeting unfolded, the CMO became defensive, insisting there wasn't enough information for them to make projections. His understanding of his role and what his responsibilities were in the sales strategy were at odds with having to come up with these kinds of concrete numbers. Without those projections from marketing, the VP of sales wasn't able to provide projections. If they didn't know what would be coming into the funnel from all the different marketing campaigns, they couldn't predict the number of appointments they would get, how many of those appointments might close and what revenue that would generate. So, if marketing didn't see themselves as having a role in that funnel at all, the system couldn't move forward because leadership could not justify the expense.

Visualizing How Sales and Marketing Share the Funnel

The Sales Placemat:

Roles & Responsibilities
Sales Process
KPIs & Performance Management

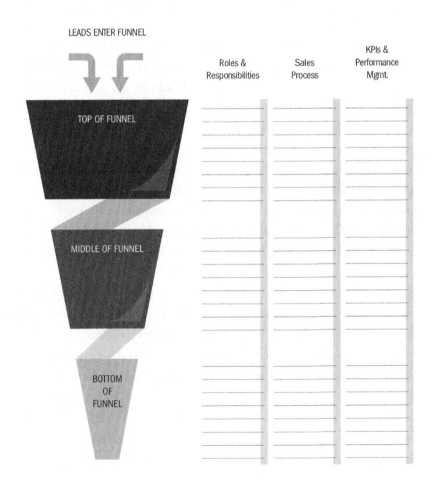

Situations like the one at Property Management Analytics highlight how necessary it is to clearly map individual team member responsibilities to the integrated sales and marketing funnel. What we call the Sales Placemat creates a rallying point, an organized framework for growing revenue and a space where sales and marketing can collaborate on individual tasks and plan their processes. Building out a Sales Placemat can help both departments see what a difference their contributions make in the company's revenue. It demonstrates the whole continuum of the sales funnel from lead acquisition to cultivation and ultimately to closed deals.

Without agreement on this framework, it is hard to get the clarity you need to get people into action. When the placemat is used correctly, not only is there more teamwork within departments but there's also the ability to set priorities, make sales projections and run reports. Processes become informed enough that nobody has to pull random numbers out of the air.

Integration means more than smoothly handing off tasks from one department to another or aligning your benefits-centric messaging. As demonstrated in the previous chapter, the sales team has the advantage of recognizing what individual customers need firsthand and which messaging tactics do and do not work. If they can properly communicate those observations within the sales and marketing team, marketing can then expand this message to reach many people. However, to scale communication from individual interactions to a large pool of customers, marketing must recognize their role within the integrated sales funnel and construct their tasks in a way that supports the ultimate end of that funnel: closed business.

To create sales projections that direct sales strategy, quantitative information must be a focus for both the sales and marketing teams. Sharing numbers as a team can remove the risk of "blame" from one department to the other, since everyone has the knowledge available to them to change course. If sales and marketing can study the sales numbers together, they can more efficiently identify where in the funnel sales leads are getting stuck and adjust processes according to whoever owns that section of the funnel and make sales projections accordingly. **If sales and marketing are approached in this way, it isn't anyone's fault that leads are stalled. Instead, it's a clear opportunity to do better.**

The benefit of working together within the sales funnel structure is you don't have to guess whether your processes and tactics are working or not. With the metrics you keep and share based on activities within the funnel, you can point to spots where the data shows your process stalling or breaking down. You can also see where your process is shining, and celebrate these wins together as one, integrated team.

How Marketing Can Operate with a Sales-Oriented Mindset

Many marketing pros are focused on numbers, analytics, branding and other key parts of marketing, but the best marketers are also customer advocates. Marketing superstars get inside customer heads to understand the pain they are looking to avoid and the goals they are looking to achieve. Fortunately, sales has a direct line to the customer and can keep marketing informed when it comes to targeting the right people and telling them the things they need to hear. Better yet, marketing teams do not have to guess how to cooperate with the sales team—they can just ask! Communication ends up making top-of-funnel leads stronger and increases conversion rates throughout the sales funnel.

Avoid Waste with Sales-Centric Marketing

To cultivate a sales strategy–oriented mindset, marketers should also consider the cost of marketing to the company's bottom line. If money goes further with good communication between departments and a clear understanding of who to target, the opposite is also true. Many marketers approach the top of the funnel with a quantity-based approach (the more leads get in there, the better!), sometimes without the deeper consideration of how likely or unlikely those leads are to make a purchase.

Use Targeting Tools for Better-Quality Leads

Marketing teams have plenty of tools at their fingertips to bring in leads. Most social media and ad platforms have at least basic targeting abilities, but some companies aren't making full use of them. We've seen many companies who haven't implemented geo-targeting and end up getting subscribers from China, Russia and other countries that aren't within their target audience. Ignoring filters and targeting functions is an invitation for spammers to bloat your email lists and skew your website traffic, confusing your metrics and making it difficult to figure out who can be moved closer to a sale. Use tools like the Amazon Reporting System and Google Search Console to hone your lead targeting (we provide more details about these tools in chapter twelve).

Value the Sales Team's Time and Skills

We mentioned in chapter two how teams can make the mistake of using an "if you build it, they will come" approach to selling. The false belief is that if you have a great product and perhaps a great website, customers will buy based on those merits alone. We also emphasized, in chapter five, how leaders must realize that salespeople have a unique set of valuable skills. However, leaders are not the only ones who need to understand these facts. The marketing team must also build up a respect for the sales team's skills and abilities and value the time and expertise that goes into nurturing a lead into a customer. With good sales and marketing alignment, including mutual respect for one another's contributions and time, marketing has the potential to set the sales team up for more success than they can achieve individually.

Realtor Sales Skills served only professionals in the real estate field who were in the United States. Their salespeople allocated a forty-five-minute window for each new business appointment, giving themselves fifteen minutes after their appointments to document their call notes in the CRM, set up next steps and calendar activities and prepare for their next appointment. Around internal meetings, the usual activities in a workday, cultivating leads and doing follow-up calls, most salespeople could only schedule four to five new business appointments per day. While this may seem like a lot of capacity to some, especially with a six-person sales team, about 10 percent of new appointments would be from outside the United States and another 10 percent would be individuals without their real estate license. That is one in five appointments that didn't meet the company's qualification criteria—which translated to 20 percent inefficiency for each sales persona, inefficiency ad spend and time the salespeople couldn't get back.

While throwing out a huge net to catch as many leads as possible might seem easier, it will result in frustration, higher costs and more confusion as you work to make sense of who is in your funnel. Using data to bring more qualified people in and keep unqualified people away will make everyone's time more valuable and raise both morale and ROI. **Plus, with alignment between the sales and marketing teams, marketing does not have to simply guess what kinds of leads are more likely to reach that final step in the funnel.** Salespeople spend time speaking with leads and can offer qualitative data to help marketing teams get out of their own heads and into the psyches of their customers. Marketing teams can use that in combination with their quantitative data to remember and reach the real people behind the numbers that make up leads in the funnel.

How Sales Can Operate with a Marketing Mindset

As we've established, salespeople have unique insight into what customers want and need. Their knowledge of the work marketing does at the top of the funnel is invaluable to their ability to multiply their success. Here are a few ways salespeople can closely align themselves with what the marketing department is up to.

Understand the Nature of Online Research

People get started on their buyer's journeys with the information they find online. Sometimes, what they find is the biggest factor in their decision, and a lead may show up already prepared to buy. Knowing what is on the website and in marketing emails and other materials can help salespeople anticipate where a lead is on their buyer's journey. That way, the salesperson knows what to say and what gaps to fill to be the catalyst to closing the sale.

Consider How Leads Want to Be Contacted

Some people prefer to be contacted via email while others prefer to talk on the phone or through video calls. Those preferences can be determined by using marketing software that lets the customer decide what they prefer. Once that information is collected via marketing, salespeople can act on it accordingly.

For example, a former client was getting ten to fifteen inquiries a month through an online pop-up form. The form collected email addresses, then sent a response to the lead with the CTA "Give us a call at this number." Nobody was following up with the leads who had entered their email addresses into the form! Only the leads who preferred to speak on the phone were closing the communication loop. There was an opportunity for the sales team to follow up with people who preferred email contact that was not being taken advantage of.

Value Customer-Focused Content

While it's vital that marketing team members understand the value of touting benefits over features (which we discussed in chapter eight), salespeople must be just as aware. One easy way to use marketing tools and knowledge is to evaluate what marketing content is getting the most attention from customers. Salespeople can use the quantitative data on which web pages get the most visits, what types of lead magnets get the most downloads and what other resources are being used most often. That data and the content it reflects should be top-of-mind for the sales team as they consider how best to help answer customers' lingering questions.

Building Intentional Sales Strategies and Tactics

Most companies are haphazard in their approach to sales and marketing. They sit their salespeople down in front of the phone and tell them to sell or tell their marketers to start posting on social media. Sales and marketing integration requires communication, and when everyone is bringing their best to the table, informed approaches to reaching leads and closing sales can much more easily emerge. Everyone should know what is happening at each stage of the sales funnel, and from there they can determine their place and duties within it.

It's marketing's job to prime a lead to learn more about your company and your offerings. Salespeople are guides who interact with those leads once they're ready. The way in which the sales team interacts with leads requires intentional design to provide those leads with what they need to continue on their journey toward becoming customers. This intentional design represents your sales strategy; the actions and tools your salespeople use to guide the leads on this journey are your sales tactics.

All good strategies should be built with the end in mind. In the case of sales strategies, the outcomes are always the same: closed deals with new or returning customers. But strategies aren't as simple as "closing more customers" and "growing more profitable." Instead, strategies require a thorough understanding of the different buyer's journeys that your leads experience and what is important to them as they evaluate your solution.

Well-designed tactics, in turn, align with your leads' wants and needs as they take each of those steps. As you develop the tactics your sales team will use to effectively guide your leads to a purchase, it's important to interact with leads to learn what they're thinking about and where they are in their decision process. With the right strategy and the right tactics, your sales team can become highly effective guides who deliver consistent, scalable results.

Factors of Sales Strategy Design

An intentional sales strategy is important, and there are many options for reaching different leads. The marketing and sales teams both must be involved in plans to target, organize and track these leads from the top of the funnel to the bottom. Consider the following.

1. **Lead Sources:** Start by aligning your strategy with each of your lead sources (e.g., lead magnet downloads, webinar registrations, contact form submissions, inbound phone calls, scheduled appointments). Each lead source will have primed the leads in different ways and to different degrees. Meeting leads where they currently are in the process enables the team to deliver the right message at the right time and improve the team's performance. By recognizing the origin of each lead, sales and marketing can more effectively communicate what that lead needs to further their understanding of your value and best determine if and how soon they want to purchase your solutions.

2. **Lead Categorization:** Develop strategies and tactics that fall into each of these common lead categories.

   □ **Education:** Leads looking to learn more about your company and your offerings

   □ **Solutions:** Leads looking to learn more about your solutions and how they differ from other solutions in the marketplace

☐ **Purchase:** Leads considering a purchase and looking to learn more about the next steps

Lead categorization provides sales and marketing with additional insights into how to best guide leads into and through the sales funnel.

3. **Lead History:** Knowing how long most leads are in your sales funnel before they make a purchase helps your sales and marketing team more accurately forecast revenue and provides benchmark data to compare and contrast with the performance of new strategies and tactics (e.g., how your leads interact with marketing materials correlated to how many make appointments to talk to a salesperson). Knowing each lead's history of interaction with your company provides insights into their interest level, which can help you develop highly impactful sales strategies and tactics.

For each strategy, consider the most appropriate tactic. For example, an automated email sequence (created and planned by marketing content writers with sales team's input) with a CTA to book an appointment with a salesperson might be the right tactic after a lead downloads a magnet. A personalized email from a salesperson followed up with a call might be the most appropriate tactic after a lead attends a webinar (planned and hosted by the marketing team).

What matters most is coming into alignment as an integrated team on how these leads will be sorted. Leads from different sources or ones that are sorted into different categories may have completely different buyer's journeys from one another. Sales and marketing need to come together to plan those journeys and make sure there is consistency between the value you offer leads at the top of the funnel through what they receive when they buy.

Integration and Feedback Lead to Impactful Strategy

Here is an example of how sales and marketing alignment led to an improved process that the team frequently used to nurture leads. Realtor Sales Skills regularly held twenty-minute group informational calls hosted by a rotating member of the sales team for top-of-funnel leads to learn more about the company's services. With a time commitment that low, it presented low risk and high value for the leads who attended, but attendance was not as high as sales and marketing leadership were hoping. To increase attendance, the team decided to further personalize their approach.

Automated pre-call email sequences were replaced with personal emails from a salesperson to leads who had signed up for each call. And these personalized emails weren't created in a vacuum. Before they went out, marketing reviewed them to make sure brand voice was congruent with the top-of-funnel messaging, cycling on the content until it was aligned with what the prospective customer had heard from the marketing team. Aligning content between departments and supporting one another makes everyone's job easier, and it makes your company look more professional and appealing to the leads you have in your funnel.

Build a Sales and Marketing Toolbox and Train Your Team

If you're going snow skiing, you need specialized equipment and know-how before you even step foot on the top of the mountain. The necessary equipment and skill set will not be the same if you go water skiing. In the same way, every different campaign your sales and marketing team tackles is going to require its own set of tools and skills.

As you develop strategies and tactics, you need supporting collateral, email and talk track templates and defined sales processes. You'll also need to ensure that sales is working with marketing, operations and IT to develop these resources. Consider these collected resources as a sales toolbox for easy maintenance and updates and routinely train your entire team to adopt and uniformly use these tools so it becomes and remains a habit.

Building this sales toolbox and training sales team members to use these critical resources will greatly increase the sales team's confidence while improving ROI on marketing and lead capture efforts. Be sure to document and evolve all best practices and standard operating procedures. Understanding every step in the sales process for different kinds of leads can create a strong competitive advantage for your company and result in shorter sales cycles, a higher-performing sales team and substantially higher close rates.

Use (and Share!) Data to Increase Close Rates

We have discussed how sales and marketing teams, in general, have access to different types of data. **Like the construct of left- and right-brain hemispheres controlling logic and creativity, respectively, a sales and marketing organization needs both quantitative and qualitative data to be whole.** It helps build an accurate picture of who is entering and moving through the integrated sales funnel and how to evaluate the lead's progress throughout. Sharing and comparing the data is what drives sales and marketing alignment and success.

Teams need to pool their learnings so that each strategy and tactic implemented has associated quantitative and qualitative data to evaluate its effectiveness. KPIs also require intentional design and should be developed at the same time you build each strategy and tactic. See the following table for examples of quantitative versus qualitative data.

Quantitative Data	Qualitative Data
• Lead Populations	• Lead Quality
• Click-Through Rates	• Education or Offering Knowledge
• Conversion Rates	
• Email Open Rates	• Interest Level or Excitement
• Email Hyperlink Click Rates	• Gut Feel or Observed Trends
• Email Response Rates	• Conversation Quality
• Call Engagement Rates	• Lead Feedback on Assets, Magnets and Resources
• Call Response Rates	
• Average Sales Cycle Timing	
• Close Rates	

Be sure to review this data together on a regular basis in sales and marketing team meetings to share knowledge and act in a collaborative, integrated way. We share more detailed information on gathering and evaluating that data as an integrated team in chapter fifteen.

The most important part of sales isn't a single strategy, tactic or process—it's the culture created among the sales and marketing team. Salespeople are the eyes and ears of every organization, and they can provide essential, game-changing feedback to leads and to the organization. They understand the potential for success and know how to close deals. The more their strategies, tactics and processes are built with purpose, the better they perform.

Developing sales strategies and tactics that align with each type of lead can unlock tremendous untapped value. To create the greatest advantage, the sales team must share its vision with the marketing team—and the marketing team needs to be ready to hear what they have to say. Integration of these teams will boost the overall performance and cooperation of both departments, ultimately generating a higher performing revenue engine for your company.

Action Items

- Use the Sales Placemat as your guide for tracking each lead's buyer's journey, what tasks take place at every touchpoint, who is responsible for them and how they will be tracked. Apply this visualization to each individual sales funnel you create for different types of ideal customer personas or leads that have been grouped using other techniques.

- Encourage marketing to value a sales-oriented mindset by recognizing how good sales strategies avoid wasted time and money, carefully identifying and targeting high-quality leads and valuing the sales team's time and skills.

- Encourage the sales team to operate with a marketing mindset by understanding the nature of a lead's online research, considering how leads want to be contacted and listening to and sharing customer feedback with the marketing team to create more customer-focused content.

- Create individualized strategies and tactics for the different types of leads marketing provides to the sales organization. Organize them by lead sources, lead categorization and lead history.

- Build your sales toolbox and corresponding sales team training for every sales and marketing tactic you employ. Use the Sales Placemat as a guide to determine who should be creating the content needed for outreach to the lead, who is creating automations, who will be following up and what metrics to use to determine the effectiveness of your efforts. Make sure to put the content you will be using in a central location and every relevant person on the team has access to it.

- Define the key sales and marketing data you would like to track for each strategy and tactic and then work with your operations or IT department to capture that data and generate reports.

Chapter 12:
Structuring Marketing Milestones and Touchpoints

Use digital marketing tactics to implement and manage sales funnel strategies.

In this chapter, we discuss a winning digital marketing strategy and how creating clear marketing milestones and touchpoints will get you much further through the funnel than winging it. We also show you how sales teams can contribute to building the structure for digital marketing processes, a contribution often ignored by marketing teams.

The internet has dramatically changed how the integrated sales and marketing funnel works. In the past, a salesperson had to ask probing questions to uncover what a lead wanted and how to educate them on the company's offers. Today's leads have done their homework, and sales and marketing must be prepared to speak to their very educated questions and requests.

Because leads experience so much of a brand online, you up the chances of being their top choice when you make their experience rich and structured. This means creating a series of touchpoints where you contact them with the right information at the right step in their journey. Effective touchpoints will guide leads from one established milestone to another, which are key parts of the funnels you want your leads to pass through on their way to eventually buying from you.

Understanding the purpose of digital marketing in relation to the sales funnel and continually modifying processes to meet the needs of prospective customers—both those who have yet to enter the funnel and those within—results in higher lead conversion rates and increased sales. In this chapter, we show you examples of how you can use digital marketing touchpoints to move leads through the funnel as well as how both sales team members can interact with digital marketing tactics to best manage leads.

Creating and Optimizing Your Digital Marketing Processes

Digital marketing is used to nurture prospects through their online research and generate qualified leads for the sales team. It creates awareness within an audience before nurturing them and moving them toward a sale. Digital marketing processes should be set up in a way that best aligns to the journey a lead goes on from the top of the funnel to the bottom, which if designed correctly, also positions the sales team for success.

In the past, it was up to the sales team to find prospects and qualified sales leads and then close them. Not anymore. Digital marketing, when done correctly, helps prospects find your company and understand why they should do business with you. These tasks do a lot of the heavy lifting before salespeople even enter the picture.

Unfortunately, many marketers don't recognize the interwoven connection between marketing and sales. They don't see the profound impact they can have on lead generation by creating opportunities for customers to interact with your company anonymously online before those customers are ready to talk with a sales rep.

Digital marketing has the opportunity to create an online path prospective customers take from their first experience of your brand, products or services through to purchase. Let's take a closer look at how to create and optimize your digital marketing strategies to make that path clear and easy to follow.

Step One: Prioritize Digital Marketing Channels and Content

Assume you already have a solid marketing strategy, excellent content and professional branding elements. The first step in your digital marketing process is to understand the content channel and content type preferences of your targeted prospects (i.e., the people who you would like to bring into your sales funnel). Where do your prospects go to get content, and what types of content do they prefer?

To answer these questions, try to understand how your target market uses the internet to research your products and services. Don't fall into the trap of thinking that just because you like a particular channel or prefer a certain way of consuming content that your audience will feel the same way. Instead, determine what they like themselves. Talk to your customers (not just your sales reps) about where they like to spend time online. You might be surprised.

Also take into consideration the purpose of each platform. Do people need a little extra help figuring out how to use the products or services you offer? A video platform could be the perfect place to offer tutorials. If you are looking for an audience who is more interested in reading content, though, video might not be the best outlet for you. As another example, a former client, who considered themselves part of the manufacturing industry, also created beautiful architectural pieces. After asking his clients, he discovered that many of them used Pinterest, a social media platform many professional and hobbyist interior designers use for inspiration. Focusing on this platform ended up being a great way to show off his unique work to the people who were most likely to buy from him.

Remember, when you align with your audience, you get better-quality leads who move faster through your funnel. Meeting them on the channels where they spend the most time and providing content appropriate for that channel create the most efficient way

to do it. Think of it like this: You must have your content available where people congregate online. You also want to have your content available in the preferred format of your target market. Some people love videos while others like podcasts. The most common way people take in content online is through written content, especially headers and taglines.

Content Channels: Here are some ways your prospects may choose to research their needs and interests on the internet.

- Market- and industry-related websites

- Association and conference websites

- Social media websites such as LinkedIn, Facebook, Instagram or TikTok

- Video sites such as YouTube or Vimeo

- Published articles, e-books and white papers

- Company website

- E-newsletters

- Reviews from sites like Amazon, Trustpilot, Yelp, etc.

Content Types: Here are some examples of content types your prospects may prefer.

- Website content

- Blog posts

- Short and long format video

- Webinars

- E-books

- Podcasts

Of course, you won't be able to cover every channel and content type, so start with the top five channels and content types and make sure you have a strong presence in each one. This also creates an opportunity for you to factor different lead sources into your sales strategy design, as discussed in the previous chapter. When you start strong with digital strategy, you get a jumpstart on building touchpoints within the sales funnel especially crafted to appeal to the unique characteristics of each segment of your lead population.

Step Two: Detail Your Digital Lead Nurturing Process

After selecting the channels and content types, the next step is to determine the paths prospects take within each of these areas. Work to understand the touchpoints, or places where prospects will interact with your brand.

Start by listing the touchpoints of your digital marketing process in order of importance. We've listed ten possible digital marketing touchpoints along the sales funnel, with the most valuable bottom-of-funnel touchpoints occurring lower on the list.

1. Website visit: home page (general company information)

2. Website visit: services and products pages (offering details)

3. Referrals from an associated website (i.e., one where your target audience spends time)

4. Social media visits

5. Follow on social media

6. Website visit: thought-leadership resources and blogs

7. E-newsletter sign-up and email nurturing

8. Webinar attendance

9. E-book download

10. Conversation with a salesperson

Each of these touchpoints should trigger specific next steps and should include clear CTAs so prospects can reach out to a salesperson when ready. In addition, note that prospects often jump around in the process, meaning that these steps won't necessarily occur in order. Be prepared to go where your prospects go, accompanying them digitally wherever they are (or are heading) in the process.

Step Three: Set Conversion Points and Funnel Touchpoints

Conversion points are when prospects go from being anonymous to connecting with your company by sharing their contact information or reaching out in another way or when a known lead (already in your funnel) completes a CTA. Here are a few examples in no particular order.

- Contact submission form

- E-newsletter sign-up

- Demo or free consultation

- Live chat

- Social media follow or like

- Blog subscription

- E-book or PDF download request

- Webinar or workshop sign-up

- Phone call to your company

- Email to a sales rep

CTAs, in turn, are the buttons or navigation links on your website that motivate prospects to do something or make contact. Here are a few examples of CTAs:

- Speak to an expert

- Get a free audit

- Get a free demo

- Get a free trial

- Buy now

- Start growing sales

Step Four: Establish Data and Analytics Tracking

You can and should use Google Analytics or a marketing automation tool like HubSpot to track the digital marketing steps you've mapped to your sales funnel, including landing page visits, email sign-ups, social media engagements and webinar attendance. It's important that you track all of your conversion points; it's nearly impossible to make informed decisions and adjust your sales strategy without providing data tracking. We'll talk more about data reporting and tools like HubSpot in chapter thirteen.

How Salespeople Can Engage and Assist with Digital Marketing

Just because digital marketing is mostly the responsibility of people within the marketing department doesn't mean salespeople can't use digital marketing touchpoints. In fact, these touchpoints can be a vital part of nurturing

Karl had an engagement with United Events, a company that produces live, hybrid and digital events. Amy, a salesperson at United Events, had been reaching out to prospects personally via LinkedIn and connected with someone who was interested in the company's services. She had a successful appointment with this contact before they decided to choose another option.

"I'd still like to keep you in mind for the future," the contact said.

Many salespeople would probably respond with a polite "OK! We may or may not see you again someday!" However, Amy recognized there was a way to keep the contact engaged with their brand so they would be top-of-mind for upcoming events. She asked if she could sign them up for the company newsletter, and once she got permission, the contact was connected to United Events' digital marketing processes. They were bumped back into an earlier stage of the funnel, but they hadn't been bumped out of it completely.

Being aware of what resources are available as digital marketing touchpoints gives salespeople tools for making the most of leads who come into the funnel at a lower point but are still not ready to buy. It's another of the many reasons integration is essential.

An Example of a Digital Marketing Process

Following is an example of a series of touchpoints that demonstrate how digital marketing processes can accelerate leads through the sales funnel. These touchpoints reflect ways in which people may interact with your brand on the internet, and they need to be customized based on the content types and channels most relevant to your prospects. We also demonstrate examples of where a salesperson might use these touchpoints to keep a lead engaged with a company or brand.

Touchpoint One: Research Resulting in a Website Visit

Your anonymous prospect is looking for a solution your product or service could provide. They'll probably start with research—a Google search, industry articles, product and service reviews or an ad click. At this point, the prospect has not made contact.

Some non-negotiables: your website must have an intuitive design, include engaging content and provide compelling CTAs to motivate lead conversion. And remember, you can't actively nurture leads until they share contact information with you.

Touchpoint Two: Social Media Visit and Follow

Once prospects follow your social media pages, you can start marketing to them using social media content. Social media is often effective at getting prospects to attend an event like a webinar or seminar. It's also an excellent way to stay in touch with lots of prospects. However, social media has its limitations, and it can be a challenging way to drive lead capture and sales. It can be an excellent top-of-funnel way to grow brand awareness, but don't count on prospects converting from social media in large numbers.

Services or Products   Resources   About   Contact

Banner Image or Video

Clear and Direct Tagline

CTA 1 - Middle of the Funnel (Learn More)

CTA 2 - Bottom of the Funnel (Get Started)

BENEFITS SECTION

Three to five clear benefits. How do your services or products add value? How are they better or different from your competitors?

SERVICES AND PRODUCTS SECTION

Three to five featured services or products. Product websites must be visual using product photos and services websites must be descriptive using content and images and/or icons.

THE PLAN OR PROCESS

This section reviews the steps to get started. This is very important for service companies. This section informs people on the steps to get started.

Step One: Discovery
Step Two: Plan Development
Step Three: Build Out and Delivery
Step Four: Follow-up

SERVICES AND PRODUCTS SECTION

Three to five featured services or products. Product websites must be visual using product photos and services websites must be descriptive using content and images and/or icons.

TESTIMONIALS SECTION

This section includes testimonials, client logos, case studies and examples of completed work. This is where the website user makes the connection between your products and services and the people and companies who buy them.

RESOURCES SECTION

This includes highlights of key resources not a part of products or service information, such as blogs, videos, e-books, webinars and other content.

BOTTOM OF PAGE CTAS

The CTAs from the banner are repeated here at the bottom of the page. In some cases additional CTAs can be placed throughout the web page.

Touchpoint Three: E-newsletter Subscription

Those who sign up agree to share their email address, which may be their personal or work account (so don't rely on domain names to know what business a lead comes from). They're letting you know they value your content and want to hear from you, so this touchpoint is an important one. At this point, the prospect becomes a lead.

This is also the point where a salesperson could easily place a sales lead within the digital marketing ecosystem, as Amy did in our example. If a sales lead isn't ready to buy when they reach the bottom of the funnel, keeping them engaged with the brand is as easy as having them provide their email address.

Touchpoint Four: Gated E-book Download

This is another point at which the prospect has expressed interest in your content and is willing to give you their contact information. However, downloading an e-book will tell you more about what solutions a lead is searching for than a newsletter sign-up will. This big step should lead to more targeted need- and value-based communications and follow-up emails.

If a lead has entered the funnel from the top, it would be premature of a salesperson to be involved at this touchpoint. For example, a salesperson in the same position as Amy from United Events could provide an e-book download as a resource and valuable form of nurturance for that contact.

Touchpoint Five: Webinar Sign-Up

This touchpoint ranks higher than an e-book download because prospects who sign up are willing to meet with you virtually. When a lead enters the sales funnel either here or closer to the top of it, this is often the point where a salesperson will make personal contact with the lead. That's why alignment is so important between the sales and marketing teams. Marketing needs to be prepared, and do the work to prepare sales, to facilitate that handoff. Salespeople need to know what is involved in the webinars and who is signing up for them. That way, they know what the lead already knows and how they might interact or follow up. Access to the webinar materials themselves, as well as the data reports from analytics tracking, must be shared.

Touchpoint Six: Form Submission

A form submission usually involves a request to speak to a salesperson. At this touchpoint, many things can go wrong, and many things can go very right. A simple technical problem can result in a prospect giving up their efforts. Slow follow-up, even waiting one day, can cost business. Oftentimes, the company that responds fastest wins the business.

Karl was working with a company that had three salespeople and a sales leader that happened to be the owner. Form submissions all went straight to the owner, who would then distribute leads. The problem was the owner could not always get to dealing with them right away. He would get busy and forget, and it sometimes took precious days for the leads to be distributed. By then, it was often too late. Having forms sent to someone who has time to make them a priority is an easy step you can take to more fruitful conversions.

Team members responsible for marketing operations can support sales by ensuring leads don't fall through the cracks. For example, they can put mechanisms in place that send autoresponders with links to schedule an appointment with a salesperson. Additionally, they can verify whether the forms are working or not. It's incredibly common for bugs in contact forms to go unnoticed or forms to be sent to the wrong email address. Checking in and fixing small issues such as these can unlock the door for more leads.

Touchpoint Seven: Scheduled Call with a Salesperson

A sales call is where marketing's role in the sales funnel often ends and the sales team's work begins. Keep in mind that contacts who become stalled at this point can often remain in a place where they can be marketed to. Just because they say no to your offering now doesn't mean that they won't be interested later. Follow Amy from United Events' lead and ask if they'd like to keep in touch, and if they give permission, keep them on your email list. That way, leads continue to be nurtured no matter what.

Tracking stats and analytics is a key way of identifying where you might have technical problems or communication problems such as the contact form glitch or the delayed follow up issues we described previously. You'll have the data you need to know how you arrived at this sales call. You'll also be able to track the ROI of your efforts and measure the return in closed business.

Tools and Resources

Many excellent tools can help you set up, implement, and track digital marketing channels. Evaluate the tools that work best for your company and budget and then begin using them immediately. Companies that use marketing automation tools and make business decisions based on the tracking data produced will outperform those that don't. For our suggestions of which tools to try, refer to the resources at the back of this book.

The internet continues to drive massive marketing and sales disruption in every industry. It's also driving intense competition between companies. With so many choices available in the marketplace for many goods and services, a lead's research process can be more drawn out and difficult than ever before. Developing an effective digital marketing process to attract leads and accelerate them down and through the sales funnel to a closed sale will be critical to your ability to drive your company's growth long into the future.

Action Items

- Understand that digital marketing can bring in a lot of leads, but you must commit to it to get consistent revenue.

- Ask your sales and marketing teams if they're following you on social media. If not, ask them to do so. Make sure everyone is getting your e-newsletter too. (We bet some salespeople don't even know you have one!)

- Audit what content channels you already use and ask your team where you think they should be. Poll your employees from different generations (and get input from your customers if possible) to see the different ways they use the internet and whether you are taking advantage of the best ways to reach your ideal customers. Then, establish which channels you will focus on with your lead generation strategy.

- Any place you have a conversion point, test it with your email and see what your experience is. Ask yourself if it's a good experience for you. Have the other team members do it too and then have a conversation about whether and how it can be improved.

- Determine your conversion points and CTAs at each step of the funnel. Make sure your conversion points interact with your CRM, and make sure you know where each notification and signup goes, so the designated people on your team are seeing them.

- Get started on an e-book and webinar to best develop the middle of the funnel. Both of us have examples of e-books on our websites you can reference.

- Assign responsibility to a team member for developing and then managing each touchpoint in your digital marketing strategy.

- Set up Google Analytics and spend time reviewing it with marketing and sales leads.

- Schedule weekly digital marketing meetings with your sales and marketing teams to review your digital marketing processes including touchpoints, conversion points and actual conversions.

- Read Tom's book *Winning the Website War* for more information about using your website to optimize your digital marketing processes.

Chapter 13:
How Automation Tools Help Your Team Do More with Less

Multiply your reach and accelerate movement through the funnel by coordinating your sales and marketing technology and automation.

In this chapter, we review how sales and marketing teams align to improve results from their software tools, including the team's CRM and marketing automation tools.

The siloing of sales and marketing shows up in lots of significant ways, and one of them is how the two teams use technology. Sales teams use CRMs to collect contact information and follow up with those contacts as they get closer to buying. Marketing teams use email marketing tools, which allow automated systems to send marketing messages and content. Both systems, when used together to their full potential, can reach more leads with less effort throughout their buyer's journeys.

Both the CRM and marketing automations are invaluable when it comes to lead scoring, content, online and offline marketing and overall understanding of where leads are in the integrated sales and marketing funnel—all things you need for effective sales and marketing integration. However, sometimes those systems aren't used effectively. There are a couple reasons for this: one is they aren't well understood by the sales and marketing teams, and the other is that sales and marketing teams don't learn to use them in collaboration with one another. In this chapter, we help lay out a plan for sales and marketing to use CRM and email marketing tools to coordinate their strategy and processes.

What Is Marketing Automation?

Marketing automation is a catchall phrase given to software applications that engage with prospects in the funnel based on those prospects' online actions, such as opening an email or visiting a web page. The automations are set up to send targeted email messages based on the user's actions. Nurturing leads using these automations allows companies to target and communicate with customers in their CRM or database in a highly effective way. Team members also benefit, as they don't have to remember to watch every lead, look for leads interacting with content or send emails to individuals manually to move them through the funnel.

Marketing automation software, such as HubSpot, makes it possible to multiply the effects of being attentive to a lead in ways no marketing team or sales rep can possibly do on their own. It allows sales and marketing professionals to be in touch with thousands of leads and send targeted messages without having to dig through email lists to look at individual open and click-through rates. It also provides the performance management data needed to score leads as they move through the funnel. These scores can trigger other automated activities and targeted actions by the sales team for a personal follow-up.

At a time when leads often want to research their purchases anonymously, sending automated content allows leads closer to the top of the funnel to learn about a company's products and services without speaking to a salesperson. Marketing automation serves leads by building awareness, helping them consider the benefits of choosing a company's solution and positioning them to make a buying decision. It serves integrated sales and marketing teams by freeing up their time to take on higher-value, more individualized tasks with leads deeper in the funnel.

If marketing sets up their automations correctly, the sales team can also benefit from all that saved time and energy. By providing useful content to leads at appropriate points in their buyer's journeys, salespeople will need to do less work educating leads. They'll have the opportunity to be proactive if they have more time to interact with leads who have learned enough about the company to better understand what they want. This serves organizations by aligning the sales and marketing process with the actual buyer's journey, thereby accelerating closed deals and revenue growth and making any marketing spend more efficient.

How Integrated Sales and Marketing Teams Use Marketing Automation and CRM

Marketing automation and CRM integration are tangible ways that sales and marketing can align their work. Traditionally, a CRM has been a contact management system, used to store information about a company's contacts, schedule follow-up appointments with them and organize all the possible sales opportunities in the funnel. Marketing automation integrated with the CRM makes automated follow-ups and supercharged data possible. Historically, almost none of the clients we work with have taken full advantage of the union between these tools. The ideal state is using these two technologies together, putting leads through the paces of an automated marketing process, entering them into the CRM and enabling the lead scoring that helps you evaluate their progress through the funnel.

A Tale of Marketing Automation and Two Guitar Companies

Fender and Gibson are two iconic American guitar companies and brands. Both have a rich history and excellent products and are staples for any guitarist, professional or amateur. However, the way they approach marketing automation is very different, and the difference is reflected in their sales and current business success.

Go to the Fender website and you quickly become immersed in the product offerings with a mix of great product photos, lifestyle images and tips from the pros. Sign up for the Fender email newsletter and you are quickly sent customized messages based on what products you've browsed on their website or bought.

Gibson sends emails promoting a demonstration video or random product that has no connection to the user's individual experience on the website. Often, the emails don't feature a range of products and are usually focused on Gibson events or artist promotions, which don't connect to a wide range of buyers or with the preferences of most guitarists. Gibson filed for bankruptcy in 2018 and is working to recover. Fender is going strong with solid sales during this same period.

Sales of guitars exploded during the COVID-19 pandemic, and Fender benefited with marketing automation that increased sales and met the needs of their loyal guitarists. What mattered the most was how they were able to use automation to segment their audiences, show those segments information most relevant to them and use their technology to see serious sales results. This worked for them much better than sending out blasts of generic content to all subscribers.

Use Drip Campaigns

One major type of marketing workflow is a form of email communication referred to as a drip campaign. Drip campaigns are emails used to stay in touch with prospects during their buyer's journey. These campaigns are email follow-ups triggered by the actions leads take and tailored to appeal to where they are in their buyer's journey. These drip emails are one of the most common and effective forms of automation.

When there is alignment between the email message and the interests of the lead, effective sales and marketing integration will amplify the impact of these campaigns.

Before we start discussing how you might create your marketing automations, remember that your leads are not all the same. You may have different marketing segments you sell to (leads grouped by source, category or history, for example), and within each segment you may have different types of personas. You also have the added complexity of understanding what is important to each one of them and where each of them is in their own buyer's journey. For this reason, one series of automated emails won't be the magic bullet that solves all your communications challenges and drives sales. You will greatly improve your team's chances of success and drive more revenue if you put in the extra work of understanding your lead and where they are in the funnel. Content carefully constructed just for them is far more effective than a series of generic, automated messages. If you need a reminder of how to build buyer's personas and their journeys, review chapter seven.

To make your automations successful, use different combinations of automations that align to your lead's characteristics and where they are in your sales funnel. Following are a few examples of aligned marketing drip campaigns that are basic but still do heavy lifting for your sales and marketing team.

- **A sign-up indoctrination sequence:** Once a person signs up for a newsletter or downloads an e-book, this sequence of emails gives them some form of introduction to a company's offering (and brand personality too). It should also wow the prospect by giving them a series of digital gifts as well as presenting a series of easy CTAs, such as asking them to follow your company on LinkedIn. When done effectively, this automation prepares your lead to expect certain communications. If you proactively show up with relevant content in their inboxes after this sequence, the fact you are fulfilling your promise will build trust.

- **A pre-webinar sequence:** When a lead signs up for a webinar, this sequence gives them information about what they will learn from it and keeps their excitement level high so they will be more likely to attend. Think of this as a primer that holds the lead's attention while providing them value and support. It also creates an additional communication channel if the lead would like to start engaging directly with the sales team before the webinar.

- **A post-webinar sequence:** This is a natural place to segment your audience, since you have two types of leads once your webinar has been held: leads who attended and leads who didn't. It enables you to send out two types of sequences that naturally align to leads who attended the webinar, and are thus more engaged and educated, and to leads who expressed interest but did not prioritize taking the next step of their journey. For attendees, your sequence might remind them of key takeaways and use cases of your solution as well as easy steps that encourage these attendees to take another step toward purchasing by demoing your solution, scheduling an appointment or moving forward with a trial. For the leads who did not attend, you may consider sending a recording (that you can track if they open or watch), another opportunity to learn more in either an active or a passive way or even a shortcut to engage with a salesperson to learn more about your solution in a more efficient and time-sensitive manner than a webinar.

There are also drip campaigns associated with parts of the buyer's journey normally handled by sales and often viewed as one-on-one communications, including:

- **Proposal follow-ups:** Once a lead has requested a proposal, a sequence of follow-up emails can be set up to automatically check in with the lead and encourage them to move forward with next steps. This can be as simple as an automated reminder email sent to a lead who has not viewed the proposal or an automation that sends if the lead has not responded to an invitation to book an appointment within a given period.

- **Post-sales-call website visits:** Even after a lead has a call with a salesperson, they may want to see more content created by marketing. Tracking the pages that a lead visits on the company website can trigger sales and marketing to send more information in the form of e-books, white papers or a marketing email sequence they may not have triggered in the earlier stages of their buyer's journey. (This is a type of digital tracking trigger that can also be considered part of lead scoring, a topic we cover later in the chapter.)

- **E-commerce sequences:** Visitors to e-commerce websites can receive multiple varieties of automated sequences based on the types of pages they visit, the products they look at and whether they have abandoned their shopping cart before purchasing. These often include discounts or other money-saving incentives that encourage the lead to take the final step to buy whatever product they've left in their shopping cart.

- **Event follow-up:** Salespeople often send sales email sequences after conducting training sessions, trade shows or other virtual events or live events. This can be an excellent way to provide value and generate ongoing engagement so you can keep your brand at the top of your target audience's mind.

Use CRM Lead Scoring for Funnel Movement and Sales Success

Lead scoring is an objective ranking of sales prospects and leads according to interest level and sales readiness. Lead scoring can help your sales team boost efficiency by minimizing the time they spend on leads who aren't interested in buying and finding leads deeper in the funnel who are ready to buy. Think of lead scoring as a way to check the temperature of your prospects.

The criteria can be explicit, such as organizing leads by industry, company and job title. The lead's online actions and behavior can also suggest implicit criteria, such as stage in the funnel, website pages visited, frequency of site visits, materials accessed or downloaded and most recent website page visits. Companies can score leads by implementing rankings such as hot, warm or cold, or A, B, C or D or a simple numerical system, 1, 2, 3, 4. Some of the more sophisticated lead scoring will use a scale of 1–10. These numbers can add up over time to give an overall score for each person in your CRM database. Generally, the higher the score, the more qualified the lead and the further along in the funnel.

What matters is everyone in the sales and marketing organization agrees on the lead scoring criteria and sticks to it. The best way to make this happen is through working together on the lead scoring process. The good news is this can be calculated and/or tracked in your CRM and marketing automation platforms like HubSpot or Salesforce.

Everything a prospective customer does online can be tracked, and marketing automation lead scoring assigns values to prospects' activities based on the criteria that you decide indicate an increased interest in your offerings or a decreased interest in your offerings. Here are some common criteria that are used to develop lead scoring:

- Number of website visits, pages visited or time spent on website

- Email opens and click-throughs

- Submission forms completed (e.g., newsletter sign-ups, e-book downloads)

- Webinar registrations and attendance

- Number of accounts set up

- Interaction with specific digital content

- Number of online purchases

- Social media activities and interactions

- Downloaded content like e-books

Prospects with higher scores can be flagged for calls and direct emails from the sales team. Likewise, prospects with lower scores can be assigned email marketing automations to help increase levels of engagement. Lead scores help you identify the value of a lead based on where they are in their buyer's journey and your sales funnel.

Watching the funnel and scoring leads helps you to never ignore leads who are ready to be converted into customers or need additional actions to accelerate the journey to becoming customers.

Use Lead Scoring to Coordinate CRM and Marketing Automations

Many teams we work with leave lead scoring to the marketing team alone. They're missing out. Lead scoring allows teams to evaluate how effective marketing automations are and assess how leads are progressing through the integrated sales and marketing funnel using an objective scale the sales and marketing teams customize themselves. The way sales and marketing teams score leads together is integral to setting up CRM and marketing automation systems, as well as deciding whether a lead may be ready to speak with a sales representative.

It is not an exaggeration to say that lead scoring is at the core of integrating your marketing automation and CRM and is the most effective way to evaluate the effectiveness of your sales and marketing efforts.

Let's say that a sales and marketing organization agrees a lead must score fifty points before being contacted by a salesperson. Every time the lead interacts with marketing content, they get a certain number of points. They may have gotten ten points for signing up for the e-newsletter, then an additional several points by regularly opening and clicking on links in those emails when they arrive. They get twenty points for signing up for and attending a webinar. At last they decide to fill out a contact form asking for more information from a salesperson, surpassing the fifty-point mark. They now have the knowledge and qualifications that make them much more likely to buy when they do interact with the sales team. If the marketing automations and CRM are connected, anyone on the sales team should see the lead's score with their contact information in the CRM and be triggered to reach out to that person via an assigned task. Without direct integration between marketing automations and CRM, and without planning how leads will be scored, leads often get stuck in the middle of the integrated sales and marketing funnel before reaching the buying stage.

Use Sales Expertise to Help Coordinate Content for Automations

While marketing teams are more by-the-numbers when it comes to measuring effectiveness of sales and marketing tactics, salespeople's work is relationship-based. Much of their data is based on real-life interactions with customers, and using those experiences to build and optimize content is a great way to write the type of emails, white papers, webinars, blogs or other informative content customers are looking for. To determine when leads are ready to pass from getting educated on a company's offers with marketing content to interacting with a salesperson, it's important to both review the anecdotal evidence and analyze the numbers.

In Karl's experience, great ideas for content have come from very structured meetings between sales and marketing. Great results have come from having the marketing team interview the sales team monthly, using targeted questions to define what solutions leads are seeking or problems they are having. It is recommended that the salespeople prepare stories of their experiences with leads over the past month in advance of the meeting to make the best use of everyone's time. You will find more advice on how to hold efficient, effective meetings in chapter fourteen.

Here are some questions that sales and marketing team members can explore together to determine what content can best prime leads to be passed from the marketing team to the sales team:

- What are the attributes of leads who show up more prepared to buy?

- What questions do leads who are most prepared to buy ask on sales calls?

- What content has leads who are prepared to buy already seen by the time they speak with a salesperson?

- What are the three questions you wish leads knew the answers to before the sales team spoke with them? In other words, what would salespeople like leads to have been educated about through marketing content before a sales call? That new content would generate leads that are more primed, more prepared and more interested in conversations about buying your solution.

If marketing is then able to use that input from the sales team to create more content, and create automations that make sure that content gets to the right leads, it can be a huge benefit to everyone. Using interactions with that content to score lead quality can ensure that leads who are unclear on the company's offerings and unprepared to discuss buying are exposed to more marketing material before talking to a member of the sales team. Salespeople do not have to spend as much time educating leads because the leads come in ready to make efficient use of their time. This type of alignment leads to mutual success for marketing and sales teams. We have found the more wins an integrated team gets under the belt, the more wins they end up creating over time—momentum creates momentum, and success is multiplied.

Use Sales and Marketing Data to Coordinate Campaigns

Because customer behavior can change for all sorts of external reasons (time of year, state of the economy, etc.) and because most businesses don't have completely static offerings, shaping automations through data analysis is an ongoing process. Over time, companies will have a variety of sales funnels and campaigns running where sales and marketing teams must coordinate content around central themes. Those may center around a season, an event, a product launch or a discount. These campaigns are a key part of driving successful automations as well.

CRM and automation let you measure the effectiveness of your individual campaigns across all channels. You can see how leads engage differently with your campaign-specific content and automations than they do with your evergreen content as well as how a current campaign compares to others. This helps you decide whether to do similar campaigns in the future or to change your approach.

Here's how data helped a private jet chartering company (which we referred to in chapter ten) get higher conversions on their marketing spend. We tested the idea that people wanting to book travel on a private jet would inquire following a Google search. We found when combining very specific travel requirements and specific seasonal travel with the search result, we could in fact generate conversion rates as high as 10 percent for private jet travel on our targeted landing pages. This worked best when the search terms in Google matched user intent. Terms like *private jet to Aspen* or *charter jet Miami* worked best because the user intent was very clear.

We also found that by using marketing automation, we could increase the conversion rate for bookings by being in front of the prospective customer when they were ready to book; their website visits and social media interactions with the company were the biggest clues to when they were ready to make their choice. The results proved that the more effectively targeted a campaign, the higher the lead conversion rate.

Develop Nurture Strategies

The type of content your leads interact with says a lot about the type of information they need to make a buying decision. An automation strategy you can use to take full advantage of your data and knowledge includes sending email content to your leads based on the pages of the websites they visit. For example, you may recall Realtor Sales Skill's ambassador program, mentioned in chapter four, where the company would connect interested real estate agents with a past customer who had gone through one of the company's programs. An automation around that program could be triggered by a lead clicking through a certain number of testimonials and case studies on the Realtor Sales Skills website.

Since not all leads are created equal, an ambassador program is not always necessary for a lead to make a buying decision. However, for a lead who is showing great interest in what past students of the Realtor Sales Skills program have to say, a chance to talk with one of them might be an offer that pushes them closer to the finish line.

Offer the Right Thing at the Right Time in the Buyer's Journey

Knowing what activities to provide at different stages of the sales funnel is vital to make the best use of everyone's time.

Here is a firsthand experience proving why offering bottom-of-funnel activities to middle-of-funnel leads can create stumbling blocks in sales and marketing efforts. Knowing each activity in the sales and marketing funnel should have a call to action guiding leads lower through the funnel, Tom decided to offer something special after a webinar: a one-on-one, thirty-minute consultation at no cost. The offer resulted in a lot of appointments for Tom but zero purchases from those leads. The miscalculation occurred because people who signed up for a webinar were still in the middle of the funnel and used to receiving free information. These leads were not yet qualified or interested enough to buy, but they were happy to get advice from Tom for free.

This same time-consuming problem happens with leads who are directed to speak with salespeople too soon. The lesson was, it would have been a better use of Tom's time if he had created automated content to advise leads in that stage of the funnel rather than take calls that were less likely to end with closed business. It's vital to plan activities in the funnel according to what leads are ready to do. If companies don't use careful planning to score leads and plan processes appropriately, they could end up with similar problems, wasting precious hours talking to people who have no interest in buying the company's product or service.

An additional level of qualifying may be needed before they speak to a sales rep. In the example, Tom dropped the free consultation from his national webinars and instead added an e-book download and videos to his website, layering on research for webinar attendees. People requesting a free consultation with Tom were now qualified to make use of what he had to say and took the initiative themselves only after the additional research.

Mapping Marketing Automation Activities to the Funnel

This is where the Sales Placemat we introduced in chapter eleven comes in handy in our efforts to map processes to the tasks they involve and the people who carry them out (you can also find a copy in the resources section of this book). You need to determine what tactics each stage of the sales and marketing funnel needs, create the right resources and communications to match those needs, decide who on your team is responsible for executing them and then come to a consensus on how you will track and score the leads in these stages. If you need a refresher on what each stage in the funnel is, what leads usually need in each stage and examples of content you could produce, review chapter nine.

To illustrate how these automations work in practice, here is an example of how marketing automation can be mapped to each stage of the funnel for a B2B sale for Plastics Inc., a manufacturing company.

Top of the Funnel

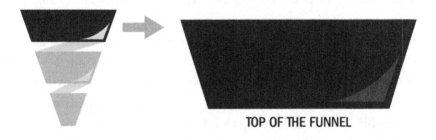

TOP OF THE FUNNEL

It all begins when a prospect, Bill from ABD Corp, visits the Plastics Inc. website. Bill reads interesting content and a case study he likes on the website, so he subscribes to the company newsletter using his company email and leaves the website.

Using Leadfeeder or HubSpot, Greg, the Plastics Inc. sales rep, can see someone from ABD Corp visited the website. Greg now has the contact information for Bill from when he signed up for the newsletter and gives him a lead score of five because of his activity.

Bill gets an email thanking him for subscribing and a PDF with a bonus case study. Over the next few weeks, he receives a series of emails as part of the sign-up indoctrination sequence to introduce him to the Plastics Inc. brand. He then goes about his work and makes a mental note to follow-up at some point.

Middle of the Funnel

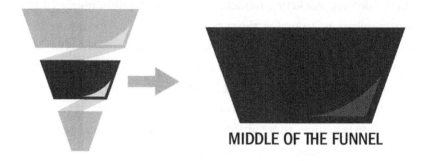

MIDDLE OF THE FUNNEL

Two weeks later, the company newsletter goes out and mentions a new certification for Plastic Inc.'s manufacturing plant. Bill takes notice because he must use suppliers with this certification to abide by the terms of his customer contracts. He visits the website to learn more about the certification, registers for an upcoming webinar and leaves the website.

Greg gets a notice that Bill has followed up and visited five website pages, spending ten minutes total on the company website. Then he notices Bill is in his lead scoring threshold for a direct follow-up email after the webinar. He gets an internal notice to follow up with a one-on-one call and personal email to everyone who attended the webinar.

In the meantime, Bill has attended the webinar but not taken any additional actions. It starts to fade into the background of his busy work life, and he mostly forgets about what he learned. Fortunately, an automated sequence of post-webinar emails reminds him about it; this sequence is specifically triggered by his action of attending the webinar. Because Plastics Inc. has a methodical approach to tracking leads through the funnel, the other automated email sequences he was receiving are turned off, so there is less noise for the post-webinar sequence to overcome. As part of this sequence, Bill receives a link to the webinar recording and watches it again over the weekend, this time giving it closer attention than he was able to during the week. He is impressed.

Next, Greg reaches out with a personalized email referencing the case study, webinar and certification. He requests a video conference call with Bill.

Bottom of the Funnel

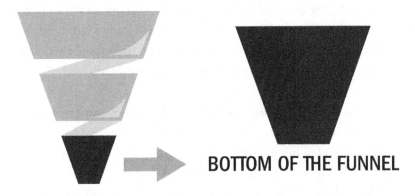

BOTTOM OF THE FUNNEL

After several email exchanges, Bill and Greg meet for a video conference. At this point, Bill knows a lot about Plastics Inc., and Greg has personally sent him additional resources via email to address his specific concerns. This makes their meeting all the more informed and powerful. After the video call, Greg prepares a proposal and soon closes a new customer. Because of Plastic Inc.'s careful automations, and because careful lead scoring set Bill apart as a higher-value lead, Greg knew just the right time and right way to reach out to Bill. This type of integration is what creates competitive advantage, and it's what allows companies like Plastics Inc. to out-market and outsell its competition.

Things to Remember When Getting Started

Companies often get expensive CRM and marketing automation tools and then end up using only a tiny percentage of the capabilities because they fail to plan carefully. It might seem time-consuming to set up all of this, but once you've got your content created and your automations set, you'll be able to start reaching a bigger audience with a more personal touch!

It is vital that you keep some things in mind:

- **Your automations are only as good as the content you produce.** Even if you have all your triggers set up correctly, boring, cookie-cutter or sloppy pieces of content will lead to unsubscribes. You need to learn about your customers and what they're looking for to start creating content that is useful to them.

- **Use marketing automation and CRM that can integrate with one another.** To emphasize how serious this is, we have seen companies fail because their information was scattered between multiple software applications that did not integrate marketing, sales and operations in any way. Don't let a preventable problem like that be how your company goes down.

- **Use a tool like the Sales Placemat to plan out interaction points, triggers, content and ownership.** This tool can get things started and get the sales and marketing teams on the same page to start evolving strategies, processes and tactics more clearly. Many CRM and marketing automation tools have features that can help teams map out automations visually to enhance collaboration, planning and execution.

Ready to select some software and get automating? Popular marketing automation tools include HubSpot, Marketo, Customer.io, Eloqua and Pardot. We're going to share why HubSpot is one of our favorites.

Why Select HubSpot for Marketing Automation?

At the time of this writing, HubSpot's software is an excellent option for marketing automation and lead nurturing, helping organizations control the entirety of actions throughout the buyer's journey. HubSpot helps thousands of companies all over the world attract leads and convert them into customers, making it the undisputed leader in the sales and marketing space. HubSpot benefits include the following:

- **All-in-one platform:** HubSpot provides marketing and sales teams a CMS, CRM, email marketing tool, social scheduling tool, SEO tool, ad tool, chat tool and analytics.

- **Email marketing:** HubSpot's email marketing tool can help you develop nurture campaigns and score contacts based on how they interact with your brand.

- **Analytics:** HubSpot analytics provide the dashboard reporting required for both inbound and outbound campaigns.

- **SEO basics:** HubSpot SEO offers the basics, along with tools non-experts can use to help track SEO keywords and improve site ranking.

- **Online support:** HubSpot online support and inbound marketing user groups and networks make it easy to understand and solve complex issues.

- **Marketing funnel:** A ready-to-use marketing funnel lets you view visitor data and analyze the impact of your marketing strategy on sales and overall performance.

As popular as HubSpot is, few organizations that use it take full advantage of its capabilities by designing campaigns for email follow-up and workflows based on the buyer's journey. Some organizations assume HubSpot will offer a quick fix to problems associated with lead outreach and lead movement through the funnel. However, HubSpot shouldn't take the place of a well-designed marketing and sales strategy; instead, it enables the solutions you develop and enables those solutions to scale.

Technology on Its Own Is Not Enough

Good technology does not equal strategy. This might not seem like news to you, but leaders will put a lot of effort into procuring the right tools and then not follow through with the preparation needed to properly get those tools to work and the team completely integrated around them.

Many organizations make the false assumption that technology alone will save the day and generate the revenue they're seeking—as if sales and revenue will materialize out of thin air once you buy the right software. How can the team find more leads? Let HubSpot figure it out. How can the team move more qualified leads through the funnel? Ask Pardot. How can the team achieve growth objectives? Let Salesforce work its magic.

Ultimately, technology is an extension of the processes your team builds, not a replacement for the efforts of skilled salespeople. The technology follows the process you develop—it doesn't magically create them for you.

Your Salespeople Aren't Robots, So Don't Expect Them to Act That Way

There are things that only a human being can do. That includes anything that requires flexibility and adaptability in the sales process. Sales and marketing managers as well as other members of company leadership need to be aware of the fluid state in which salespeople must exist.

The day-to-day life of a salesperson is ever-changing and requires the salesperson to shuffle priorities and interact with customers and stakeholders according to their individual needs. There also is a limited amount of time in which a salesperson can reach out to leads. They can't take their work home in the same way a developer, strategist or designer might. A salesperson may go to sleep and wake up to five new leads. To address those leads in a timely manner, they must be able to shuffle activities and reprioritize in a way that makes the most of the hours when it's appropriate to reach out and speak with others. An automation cannot adjust to those circumstances in a nuanced way that a human can.

The Unique Value of Human Outreach

One company Karl worked with was bringing on one hundred new leads each month through their automated marketing. Once they brought those leads into the funnel, they sent automated emails and surveys to get feedback on the content sent to the leads. The value of each new customer averaged $25,000 per year. The problem was the company was retaining only 25 percent of those leads over the next thirty days.

To raise the retention rate of these leads, Karl proposed a more hands-on approach. Instead of just emailing the leads, the sales team would try calling each lead who signed up over the next month to interview them about their needs. If no one picked up, they would leave a voice mail offering additional help. Leads who received phone calls and voice messages started responding, and the rate of retention more than doubled.

When even a well-coordinated email marketing approach doesn't yield satisfactory results, turn to your sales team to do the work the robots can't do. Even better, organize your automations so your people can work in harmony with those automations. While humans are better at adapting to shifting priorities, well-structured tech tools and lead scoring systems are instrumental in helping them assess and prioritize.

Good People and Good Tech: An Unstoppable Combination

Salespeople have a lot of nurturing to do once marketing has qualified a lead, and technology can make that much easier on them. While marketers often have a lot of ownership over the software, they can use that ownership to help make it easier for salespeople to do their jobs.

In one of the software programs we work with, salespeople can track calls they've made, the result of each call and next steps. When they make a call, they use a form that has a series of radio buttons with possible outcomes (the lead doesn't answer and the salesperson leaves a voice mail, the lead doesn't answer and the salesperson leaves no voice mail, the lead answers and agrees to speak further, the lead answers and decides they want to buy, etc.). When the salesperson is finished with the call, they indicate its outcome on the form.

In a well-planned integrated funnel, the marketing and sales team will already have defined, clear next steps based on each outcome. For example, if the lead says, "Not at this time," the salesperson might choose to put the lead back into an automated marketing system. The lead may decide later to again move down the sales funnel due to one of these automations. If requested, the salesperson could also remove the lead entirely and not take the risk of giving anyone a poor impression of the company that sends unwanted follow-ups.

Collaboration is key to marketing automations and salespeople playing in harmony. It means salespeople have the space to contact more of the right leads and make good impressions on them, upping their chances of success. For them to truly make the best use of available technology and skills, their humanity must be recognized. Leadership must allow salespeople to have ownership over tasks and processes that align to their major talents.

Action Items

- Assign a team member to evaluate marketing automation tools such as HubSpot, Marketo, Eloqua, Customer.io and Pardot. Demos, trials and sales calls with the top contenders may prove valuable here. Evaluation criteria might include cost, flexibility and scalability, ability to integrate with other technologies and ease of use. Make sure your marketing automation software combines the CRM with your marketing automation efforts. The combination of these two types of software should be able to score leads in the contact database.

- Plot out the placement of content, automations and who owns each activity, building on maps you've made for the buyer's journey and the milestones and checkpoints within it. You can use the Sales Placemat or tools provided by your marketing automation and CRM software. Depending on what type of business your company does, these funnels might be organized by product, offering or audience.

- Consider what paths your customers might take based on the buyer's journeys you have determined as well as your offerings. Knowing how people make decisions to buy helps you develop relevant content and construct email sequences based on what your leads show interest in and what criteria they use to make a purchasing decision. This will change according to different campaigns you run and according to the feedback you receive from sales team members' discussions with customers and from the data you observe in your marketing automation analytics.

- Learn more about lead scoring. If you have a marketing automation tool or CRM that enables lead scoring, use the information those tools provide to understand their lead scoring capabilities. Then work with sales and marketing teams to develop a draft version of scoring and begin to test within the tech stack of your marketing automation and CRM.

- Assign scores to each action a lead could take based on the content that is being sent to them. This helps you determine how that lead is progressing through the funnel and whether the content you send them is effective in moving them from one step to another. Decide what score leads have to reach before a member of the sales team reaches out to them, based on the amount of content they have already received and engaged with.

Chapter 14:
Sales and Marketing Meetings that Energize Teams

Bring sales and marketing integration magic to life one meeting at a time.

In this chapter, we emphasize the importance of getting leaders of both sales and marketing teams into alignment to have effective meetings. Regular, efficient sales and marketing meetings drive strategies, create action items and eventually yield positive results.

By now, you have a grasp of what you're supposed to do to use your integrated sales and marketing departments to their full potential. The best way to build those collaborative systems is to conduct effective integrated sales and marketing meetings.

Meetings are the heart and soul of sales and marketing integration. They are one of the most crucial factors in orchestrating the type of cooperation that results in closed sales. They also foster regular communication, which prevents disagreements and misalignments that can lead to conflict between departments.

Let's be honest—many company meetings waste everyone's time. They lack focus and structure, and most people leave them frustrated and wondering why they attended in the first place. This goes double for when there are already conflicts between sales and marketing.

Believe it or not, it is entirely possible to use meetings as a tool for your sales and marketing efforts to flourish. Good meetings are opportunities to source great ideas, assign tasks that will move your strategies forward and align the whole team. It just takes a combination of practical preparation, intentional execution and shifted mindset.

The Spirit and Action of Teaming

Many times we have shown up to meetings full of disengaged team members who see meetings as something to be endured and then escaped and forgotten. Even if the leader is fully engaged, they often end up just following a series of bullet points. Instead of taking advantage of having everyone in the same room to collaborate, leaders conduct one-sided conversations and lecture on decisions that they've already made without input. The meeting feels like a box to be checked rather than something that results in creative problem-solving, clear action items and an understanding of where to go next.

You can't just change your unhelpful organizational habits overnight. It takes a change in everyone's attitudes toward integrated sales and marketing meetings to start getting value. Without an initial mindset shift, you won't be able to create a meaningful and fruitful experience for the team. *Teaming* is a word we use for the action of shifting to a positive mindset and unifying around a shared goal.

The most effective way to enter productive sales and marketing meetings is to remember that you are coming together to create results, not just to dictate or to be dictated to. Meetings are spaces for team members to share observations and ideas, as well as ask for what they need to fulfill their roles in the sales funnel.

For example, let's say the integrated sales and marketing team of Realtor Sales Skills meets, and the marketing team suggests holding a new webinar to educate top-of-funnel customers. Putting forth their plans in front of the whole group gives sales team members the opportunity to chime in with how those webinars can more effectively educate and qualify leads.

"We are planning a webinar, but we're not sure what the topic should be," Naomi, the director of marketing, might say. "I spoke to my teammates in marketing, and we all are curious to learn from the sales team. What are you all hearing and seeing right now? What are some of the primary questions or objections you're getting? What do you think leads want to know as they come into a call with you?"

Sophie, a sales team member, says, "I am getting a lot of questions about how our offerings work for realtors in areas where home values have not been increasing as much as some of the hot markets. I also get similar questions about how our offerings work in rural or more non-suburban markets. I think leads just want more knowledge or assurance that our programs work no matter where they live."

The marketing team now has a new angle to use when they create content, one they know will be relevant to the sorts of concerns leads have when deciding whether to buy their courses. If they had not collaborated with the sales team with a spirit of teaming, they probably would have created content that didn't take the lead's point of view into account.

Meetings are an opportunity for teammates to bond, collaborate, and address problems that affect everyone related to your organization—especially your leads. This is the space where you solve problems together, rather than passively half-listen to what plans someone else has for you.

Meetings with No Structure Fail

While getting everybody together at the same time is an absolute must for alignment and integration to work, you need more than a winning attitude for meetings that succeed. Just like your overall sales and marketing success, meetings also live and die by strategy, processes and people. You need a strategy for how to run meetings in the first place, you need to have processes that make them efficient and useful and you need to make sure all your people are participating and gaining value from them.

When and How to Run Your Integrated Team Meeting

With all the changes occurring in your market, you need to be able to pivot your sales and marketing strategy and tactics to stay ahead of those changes and keep your competitive advantage. An integrated sales and marketing meeting should be an effective use of time. It should be flexible enough to deal with interpreting quantitative and qualitative data and still address the day-to-day challenges and triumphs your team is experiencing.

The following actions demonstrate ways we facilitate meetings to support and coach teams to make the most of their time together. Consider incorporating these fundamental enhancements to make your meetings more effective.

Preparing for a Team Meeting

Just like a good salesperson prepares for a call with a lead, running an effective team meeting doesn't happen by accident. Whoever leads the meeting must have an agenda already in place. Share any resources or assignments in advance. Also consider whether your meeting environment is primed and ready to go; this might mean having a room set for the group, ensuring whiteboards and markers are clean and new and any digital content is preloaded and at the ready.

Organizing Who Will Be There (And Who Does What)

Decide who will attend the team meeting. Don't just invite everyone. Be selective according to who will really benefit from what you will discuss. A comfortable number is four to six people; you want no more than eight if you want everyone to engage and participate fully.

Allot roles to people before your meeting starts if you will be talking about executing a particular project. For example, if marketing is starting a new initiative and wants someone from sales to help them get insights and anecdotes from real leads, it is a much better idea to select who that person will be beforehand instead of wasting time in a meeting trying to get a volunteer. Organizing yourselves in place isn't the best use of your time and will lose people's attention. It's preferable to have a brief conversation before your meeting than lose your team's attention right from the start. Additionally, if there are two people leading, to avoid hiccups, it's important to identify who will be covering what.

Equipping Your Attendees Ahead of Time

People should already know from your agenda that they won't leave the meeting saying, "That could have been an email."

Don't surprise meeting attendees with the topics of discussion. Remind them what the purpose of the meeting is, send them the agenda and invite them to add to it. You can get much more out of your meetings if people come prepared with their own questions and concerns in response to your agenda. If you are going to ask an attendee to present something, make sure you remind them well in advance of the meeting so that they come prepared, avoid embarrassment and take their role seriously.

With higher-level team members and leadership, giving them as much information as possible as soon as possible will help them feel like the meeting is worth the limited time they have to attend. It will also encourage higher-ranking members to lead by example and fully engage because they can see the rewards that this meeting can produce. Also, a bonus—reaching out far enough ahead of a meeting might even light a fire for all participating team members to tie up loose ends, run reports, write content or make calls they've been putting off but need to complete either for the meeting or in order to make time to attend the meeting.

Encouraging a Productive, Cooperative Headspace

A good meeting covers what the sales and marketing team will co-create in the future, rather than rehashing problems that have occurred in the past. Make sure everyone understands that this is a time for collaboration and construction, not for complaining. It's an opportunity to put all you know about the magic and potential of sales and marketing alignment and integration into action. Everyone should approach it with the company's values in mind and be ready to respect each other's input and ideas. They should have done any requested assignments, show up on time and give the meeting their full attention. Especially if meetings up until this point have not been productive, pointing out the need for a mindset shift can really set the tone for a new way of doing things. It primes them to be ready to work and be greater than the sum of their parts.

If you are running the meeting, it's essential to start on time and tell your audience what your role will be, where you are taking them, what they can expect and what attitude you want them to bring into the meeting. Always manage the meeting effectively to end on time. If you find yourself being taken down a detour that is off topic, set that topic aside and get refocused on the task at hand. Value comes when everyone is participating and you are working toward the goals you agreed upon.

How to Structure Your Sales and Marketing Meetings

While your meetings should have space for creativity and collaboration, all meetings must have a clear agenda to be worth everyone taking the time out of their day. Meetings also must take place regularly enough to provide everyone with useful direction. Here's the structure we have found to create useful and efficient sales and marketing meetings.

ACTION ONE: SET INTENTIONS AND CREATE CONNECTIONS

This first step is especially important to highlight if this is the first time you've brought your sales and marketing teams together. You'll need to do this on a larger scale when you begin having integrated meetings, though in each of the following meetings you will set intentions as well.

In your first integrated meeting, get consensus on what you and your team envision for a more powerful partnership between the sales and marketing departments. Just like you did when creating your buyer's journeys, use the magic wand technique to envision your ideal outcome. What would you want the sales and marketing teams' partnership to look like in a year? Really let your imaginations run free. The goal is for you and your team to share enough ideas that all of you get excited about what the ideal future state would look and feel like.

In each of your future meetings, start with determining what you will accomplish together. Focus on ideas, initiatives and actions through the lens of the team's original vision of the desired state. Hold the original vision while also intentionally laying out what big-picture goals you want to achieve from that day's topic of discussion.

To unlock the value each person can bring to your meeting, make sure you are creating connections between team members. A good way to do this is to start each meeting with a sharing activity to help everyone feel valued and included. For example, ask everyone to share a personal and professional win, a lesson learned, a recognition for a teammate or something positive they want to celebrate together. It doesn't need to take much longer than five minutes total, and while it might seem nonessential, we assure you the connection and energy it creates is well worth it.

ACTION TWO: REMEMBER WHY YOU ARE MEETING

We recommend clearly stating what the goals of each meeting are, which may vary. Objectives of some meetings we have run include sharing knowledge, connecting as a team, inspiring one another, creating accountability and getting into action. Other meetings might be more tactical, where you come together specifically to process an issue or get something done. Knowing why you are meeting, the goals of the meeting and how you want everyone to participate not only sets the stage but creates focus for you and your team.

ACTION THREE: EVALUATE WHERE YOU ARE RIGHT NOW

Whatever your specific meeting purpose, it is valuable to evaluate your current state. Where are you right now? Where is your team? Depending on the meeting type, you will use qualitative information or quantitative information (but often a bit of both) to accomplish this evaluation.

A discussion of qualitative information may include asking each teammate how they think the collaboration between the two departments is going. An example of quantitative information may include reviewing specific KPIs related to an integrated sales and marketing campaign to determine what tactics are working well and what tactics might need to be improved. This is a perfect example of why you need to properly prepare any team members who will be attending, so they will show up with the data and anecdotal information to make the best use of everyone's time.

ACTION FOUR: ALIGN ON WHERE YOU WANT TO GO

Many teams are used to weekly, rinse-repeat meetings where they can mostly tune out. When every meeting is geared toward a particular outcome, things change. This is the part of the meeting where you will explicitly name the problem, challenge or initiative you have come together to solve. This might include you or your teammates sharing any problems or concerns surrounding the initiative or any other background information that enables you and your team to have the same vantage point as you work together to move things forward.

Sometimes you will need multiple meetings to achieve the outcome you are looking for. If this is a follow-up meeting and the team has already been working on the topic, then checking in on the status in light of the desired outcome helps set the stage for determining next steps. This way, the integrated team can evaluate together whether something is working, and if not, what to do instead.

When we say outcomes, we don't just mean the overarching business outcome a successful initiative will produce, like a higher number of booked appointments after a mid-funnel marketing campaign. We are talking about multiple outcomes for each individual department—even departments other than sales and marketing. It could mean fewer unqualified leads wasting a salesperson's time, greater comradery between sales and marketing teams or more efficient product fulfillment because marketing communicated an offering more clearly. Only by examining how your goals affect everyone in the organization will you be able to assess your path forward and avoid conflict.

ACTION FIVE: CHART THE PATH FORWARD OR GET INTO IMMEDIATE ACTION
Once the team is aligned on the desired outcome or destination, it's time to generate ideas and workshop solutions. The two types of meetings we use most commonly are strategy sessions and working sessions.

Strategy sessions allow the integrated team to determine how they will get from their current state to the one they ultimately want. This could mean determining how they will create and automate marketing content around a lead nurturing activity like an email sequence sent to leads after they download a magnet. It could also mean troubleshooting how to get more success from a sales campaign that isn't getting you the results you want. In this situation, the team may use this time to clarify what tasks need to be done to carry out the strategy, who will own every task, the timeline, next steps and how your path forward will affect different departments and individuals in your organization.

An example of a working session would be having the integrated team create the individual components of an integrated sales and marketing strategy. In this situation, the strategy has been finalized and the working session could consist of co-creating a lead magnet, a webinar outline, email sequences or overall messaging. An additional example of a working session might be an educational meeting, where the team practices whatever skill-building techniques are the focus of the meeting. Giving your integrated team the chance to develop their skills gradually, including preparing data and engaging in creation and strategizing with teammates in the actual meeting, will help them be more effective over time.

ACTION SIX: PLAN NEXT STEPS & CREATE ACCOUNTABILITY

Every meeting should have clear next steps, owners, requirements or dependencies and agreed-upon schedules and timelines. Make sure all participants agree and understand what's next. If anything seems vague, now is the time to speak up and ask clarifying questions. If you are leading the meeting, check in with your team members and ensure they understand what their own next steps are.

With practice, your entire team will naturally make sure this clarity check-in is part of every meeting. This discipline creates accountability and good habits, and your meetings will be perceived as high in value to your integrated sales and marketing team.

ACTION SEVEN: ALWAYS SUPPORT COMMITMENT WITH A RECAP

Nobody should leave a meeting, no matter how positive, thinking, "That's nice, but I doubt anything will come from it." When we coach our clients, we emphasize it is everyone's responsibility to support the team and do what they have each agreed to do. This means advocating for one another, staying in proactive communication and providing meeting recaps to the entire team with action items and clearly defined owners.

This step is often overlooked, but we cannot stress its effectiveness and how important it is to do consistently. We always assume positive intent from every team member, but people get busy—there is always another meeting to attend or another fire to put out. Supporting the team through providing solid recaps builds trust, collaboration, accountability and good habits. You'll find these good habits sneak into other meetings as well (your salespeople may even start doing it after sales calls with their leads).

Whoever is running the meeting is responsible for doing everything they can to encourage follow-through. The in-person recap should be followed up by an email to spur action and serve as a testament to the effectiveness of sales and marketing working together. Without these steps, people are less likely to recognize the value of your meetings. With a clear email recap, the evidence is right there in their inboxes.

Committing to conducting your meeting according to those seven actions is an ongoing process. You can't just agree to it once and expect to see results, in the same way you can't just work out once and expect to magically be in top shape. **You need to constantly recommit to the process in order for the magic of sales and marketing alignment to take you to the levels of growth and success you want for your company.**

A Meeting Mindset Shift Will Have Consequences

Many team members will be relieved that meetings aren't boring anymore—they will finally get something useful out of them. However, engaging with a meeting is a more demanding experience for attendees who are not used to it. People are expected to contribute and collaborate; marketing needs to prepare data, and sales needs to be able to talk about their current leads. After years of pointless meetings, increased expectations and accountability can be a tough adjustment.

Some team members will have a more difficult time coping with the new standards than others. Poorly performing team members will have nowhere to hide, and the rest of the team will be able to see where the ball is being dropped. Either they will step up to the challenge after a couple of embarrassing sessions, or they will decide to find another job that demands less input.

The positive side of turning the spotlight on your team members is that many will rise to the occasion. Meetings that are more based on creativity and collaboration will engage more folks who normally don't pay much attention, and you will find amazing ideas can emerge from unexpected places. You may also find that people on your team have skills and talents they have never shared.

How Meetings Can Reveal Your Team's Authentic Selves

Karl was working with an events company, United Events, in the process of finding the right account executive to join their team. In his time together with them, they had already committed to the types of meetings just described, which require engagement and collaboration. So, when they thought they had found their new teammate in Tim, they brought him immediately into that meeting style. In their onboarding meeting with their new account executive, they asked him to interpret the company's elevator pitch and make it his own. This meeting ended up putting his personality on full display in a way the interviews hadn't.

Tim all but regurgitated what was in the company handbook. While the content was accurate, the delivery was robotic and lacked personality. The leadership team imagined they were at a networking event and Tim had just introduced himself and United Events. When they listened from the point of view of a potential lead, what Tim delivered didn't connect or feel authentic.

"We don't need you to just memorize something and be able to repeat it verbatim," they said. "We'd like you to come up with something that captures the spirit of United Events, feels right to you and connects with our audience."

The more Tim was asked to evolve his elevator pitch, the more un-comfortable he became. Unfortunately, all he could do was restate the written words from the playbook. At the same time, his enthusiasm to go to networking events or reach out to leads and tell United Events' story flatlined. He ended up quitting after just two weeks on the job.

Then there was Amy, who showed up to that elevator-pitch meeting with questions of her own. Instead of memorizing what was written in the company handbook, she dove deeper into what its words meant to United Events. She really wanted to understand what made the company unique. After she digested the answers, she personalized her elevator pitch. Amy proved she was fully engaged, and she nailed it when leadership asked her to demonstrate her own translation of the elevator pitch.

"I would tell them that as a professional, I value trust and being proactive. I make sure I do what I say I'm going to do, and I work with people who do the same," she said. "And one reason I wanted to work with United Events is because when I read about their values, I saw they were the same as mine."

When Amy was able to apply her personal filter to the company handbook's message, she owned her elevator pitch. Her enthusiasm carried over into successful networking events, outreach emails and conversations with leads. All it took was a little inspiration, and Amy was empowered to be the best she could be. When a spotlight shined on her during an intentional, productive meeting, she bloomed.

Practice and Scoring Make Meaningful Integrated Meetings

Nothing is perfect the first time you do it, and that goes for meetings as well. Don't worry if you start implementing this more engaged meeting model and things feel a little awkward. Do make sure each meeting you have improves on the last. Consider having the team score meetings on overall effectiveness and usefulness. It doesn't have to be something too official—a simple 1–10 evaluation from each person on the team should be enough. The score should be based on whether they believe the meeting outcome matched up with the stated intention. If it's not 8 or higher, we recommend getting feedback about what could have been done better to make it a This can be done at the close of the meeting, or if you feel a more private dialogue would encourage more honest feedback, you can always schedule a one-on-one outside the meeting.

Don't give up! Having worthwhile meetings is like learning to play an instrument. The more you do it right, the easier it will be.

Meetings for Sales and Marketing Managers

While everyone can be involved in evaluating the usefulness of team meetings, meetings between sales and marketing managers can be more quantitative and evaluative of the whole team's performance. This is the time when they look at the entire state of the sales funnel and funnel activities to see how effective they are. This is also where data is necessary, and it's vital you've established cooperation and information sharing between departments. We go into more detail about what types of data should be collected and reviewed in the following chapter.

Action Items

- Set up a regular and recurring meeting in a shared calendar for sales and marketing alignment. If you have them, make sure to schedule an internal meeting with the leaders of the sales and marketing departments before you bring in the entire team. Remember that prework and putting a plan in place before the first meeting will set you and your team up from success.

- Take a little time to search the web for examples of meeting formats or lessons on how to run effective meetings, especially if you're new to running meetings. See if you can find a format you like and then start to develop your own meeting outline. You may agree the format we provide is useful, or you may find another format that might work better for you.

- Remember that successful meetings are intentional. Create connections between attendees, remember why you are meeting, evaluate your current position and align on where you want to go. Then, chart your path forward, speak about the action you'll take and end with a recap and an agreement on what your next steps will be.

Chapter 15:
How to Use Sales and Marketing Data

The capture and analysis of detailed data is at the core of all successful sales and marketing efforts.

In this chapter, you learn about the metrics used in the integrated sales and marketing funnel. We will give you guidelines to determine what to measure, who should measure it and how your team can use data to optimize performance and reach sales goals.

In all our years of working with sales and marketing teams, we've never met a company who didn't want to be more successful—whether that means making more money, being more efficient or both. Pulling back the curtain on successful sales and marketing operations shows careful data tracking and evaluation driving growth in sales revenue. This data is best tracked with an integrated scorecard across all points of the funnel.

An integrated scorecard is one that includes data points from all metrics in the buyer's journey, including both traditional marketing data and the data from the CRM used by the sales team. There cannot be effective (successful) alignment of sales and marketing without an integrated scorecard to track what's working and what is not.

Companies tracking sales and marketing activities with integrated scorecards outperform those that don't. Awareness is the key to success in sales and marketing performance, and it starts with knowing the numbers and assigning responsible people to track them and make them real. **Awareness of how data can inform your sales and marketing decisions is non-negotiable for companies looking to survive and thrive in today's marketplace.**

The best-performing sales and marketing companies assign owners and targets to each part of the integrated scorecard. They also have their target numbers in place to contextualize the results they get for those different parts. If a student receives 155 points on a test, they wouldn't know whether they've gotten a good grade without knowing the highest possible number of points. If a person in charge of email marketing says their latest e-blast was opened by 155 people, they wouldn't know whether it was a good sign unless they knew how many people received the email.

It was once difficult to track such specific metrics, but with marketing automation software and CRMs, this is no longer the case. Sales and marketing performance data is now driven by detailed information about customer interactions and research. This information can be collected at every stage and step in the integrated sales and marketing funnel. It can then be assigned to people on the team as accountability points driving sales results.

Where Does Scorecard Data Come From?

Most of the data used in an integrated scorecard originates from a few key data points. Here are the most important sources of this critical sales and marketing data.

Google Analytics: This tracks all sources to a website and the activities on it. It is the central point for how users interact with your brand

and begin their buyer's journey. Data from Google Ads also can be found here.

The Google Search Console: This is the most important SEO tool on the planet and can be organized with tools like SEMRush or Moz. It collects excellent top-of-funnel data, including keyword volumes and website ranking.

Social media: Like a website visit, social media is top-of-funnel and key to building brand awareness. Each social media platform offers detailed reporting on user activity.

Marketing automation and email marketing: Scorecards are built on marketing automation workflows and activity in the CRM. Email marketing campaigns should be established in marketing automation software.

CRM software integrated with marketing automation: Key data flowing through the middle and bottom of the funnel will be found where marketing automation meets the CRM. This includes data associated with sales transactions, which may need to be aggregated from accounting software if it is not captured in the CRM.

You will make best use of these reporting tools if you set up your automations to have data flow into the integrated scorecard. There are tech tools that can do it for you, aggregating data from different sources and rolling them up into one interface for effective reporting. One of our favorites is Easy Insights, which is a cloud analytics platform that draws and displays your data on dashboards in real time, enabling you to act more quickly.

Well-Monitored Data Can Reveal Critical Errors

One of our clients ran a Google Ads campaign to send traffic to their website to convert visitors into leads and ultimately sales. The goal was to create a simple campaign to test how effective it would be to run paid search ads. Keeping it simple was a way to test the water temperature without jumping in with both feet.

The marketing team was careful and collaborative in their approach. They looked at search traffic and competitors' landing pages, sought input from the sales team and formed a keyword-based strategy. Those keywords were coordinated across the ads and the landing page the ads led to, and they aligned perfectly to the buyer's journey of the company's target audience. They had done everything by the book, and when they flipped the switch to turn on the Google Ads campaign, everyone was excited to see what would happen.

By the end of the first week, 150 leads had clicked on the ads, and between 10 and 15 percent had clicked through to the Google submission form on the website landing page. Those numbers correlated with what the team had been hoping for; however, something was not working. When website visitors reached the landing page, they were not taking the next step and completing the contact form. While not totally out of the realm of possibility, the lack of form submissions over a week didn't seem consistent with their success with the actual ad clicks.

When we dug in further, we found the company that created the Google submission form on the website had not set the permissions correctly. Leads were unable to enter any of their information into the form. Since the campaign began, leads had been clicking on the Google form, but could not take the next step. Within a week of fixing the permissions, leads started completing the Google form. The first new deal resulting from that campaign closed by the end of the month.

Judge Your Effectiveness through an Integrated Scorecard

There are many data points to track in the integrated funnel, but simply tracking how many leads enter the funnel and how many end up buying isn't enough. To truly make the most of carefully crafted marketing automations and a well-organized CRM, every team must have KPIs in their integrated sales and marketing scorecards.

Each KPI in the scorecard has a purpose, and team members should know why they are tracked. These guideposts are the foundation for measuring success and movement of leads through the funnel. The integrated sales and marketing scorecard should answer the following questions about your KPIs and data points.

Are Marketing Tactics Bringing People to the Website or Key Landing Pages?

Knowing this answer is knowing whether your marketing strategy and tactics at the top of the funnel are working. Some KPIs in this category include the following.

- **Source or channel data:** Where your website visitors come from (e.g., SEO, social media, direct website traffic, referrals from other websites, email marketing or paid search or paid social).

- **Campaign results:** The number of sessions from visitors accessing your website through tracking URLs associated with one or more specific campaigns. This tells you whether a particular lead source yields more reliable leads than others.

- **Ads and impressions:** Click-through rates, ad spends, cost per acquisition and the number of times people view or click on your ads. (Note: Be sure to track conversion rates from your ads to your conversion metrics as well, e.g., time on site, form completion or even purchase.)

- **Unique website visits and pages visited:** Number of visits to your website from unique individuals.

- **Geolocation of visitors:** Geographical locations of leads in specific countries, areas within a country, places of interest, your business locations or other tiered demographics.

- **Visits by device:** Data regarding where your traffic comes from (e.g., desktop, tablet or mobile device).

How Engaging Is the Website or Landing Pages?

It's not enough to track website visits when your goal is sales; you need to focus on measuring how they engage with the website when tracking KPIs. The goal of a website visit is solely to build interest and move people toward a conversion that captures their contact information. Engaged visitors are more likely to take the next step by downloading content, signing up for an email newsletter or webinar or submitting a contact form. The following are data points that measure whether your website inspires visitors to take that next step.

- **Page visits:** The total number of pages a visitor views during each website session.

- **Sessions:** The total number of website sessions, including repeat sessions from the same website visitor and whether they have visited before or are brand-new.

- **Time on site:** The total amount of time visitors spend on the website reading content and researching.

- **Bounce rate:** The percentage of visitors who land on a particular page of your website and then leave without visiting any other pages.

How Effective Is the Offer or CTA?

There are plenty of metrics to judge whether an offer is enticing enough to move leads to action, much more than just the final number of buyers.

- **Form completions/submissions:** The number of visitors who provide their contact details through a form or sign-up.

- **Conversion by content source:** The type of content driving conversions, such as website content, blogs, email, social content and more.

- **Conversion by traffic source:** The source and channel people use to find your CTA and then convert. Conversion rates vary by channel based on user intent and where they are in the funnel. These channels include Google, social media, direct visits, ads, website referrals, influencers and more.

- **Heat mapping:** Where visitors put their mouse on a website or landing page during a session. These metrics show which offers are most enticing. Our favorite heat mapping tool is CrazyEgg.

How Well Do Marketing Email Sequences Work to Move People through the Funnel?

There are many ways to track how effective email sequences are in moving leads through the funnel. Most email automation sequences have those metrics readily available. Here are a few KPIs to measure to analyze engagements and conversions from your email list.

- **Total emails sent:** How many emails were sent and did not bounce.

- **Email open rate:** The percentage of successfully delivered emails that recipients opened. This is a measurement of how well your subject line works and the amount of interest in your topic. Keep in mind, some emails get opened more than once, which also indicates how valuable recipients find the information to be.

- **Email click-through rates:** How many recipients clicked on a CTA in your email (usually to visit your website or a landing page). Some measure the click-through rate based on total recipient population, and others measure based on the number of people who opened the email.

How Effective Is the Sales Team at Follow-Up and Closing?

There are two primary groups of sales KPIs. The first group is based on activities the sales team performs, and the second group is based on populations.

SALES ACTIVITIES

These metrics could be based on more traditional business development and prospecting activities, which we define here as outbound sales. They could also be related to leads that are already in the funnel and that have passed from marketing to sales. With all activities, we recommend recording a lead's conversion rate to the next step of the sales process (i.e., whether the lead took the desired action). For example, you would record the number of calls a salesperson makes to leads who have attended a webinar but not yet booked an appointment, and then the conversion rates from the calls to a scheduled appointment.

Frequently measured sales activities include the following.

- **Emails sent:** The number of emails sent from sales that are associated with a specific category of lead. This could mean the number of emails sent to leads with a specific lead score or the number of leads who just entered a specific stage of the sales funnel owned by the sales team.

- **Calls made:** Similar to emails sent, this is the number of sales calls associated with a specific category of lead. This could mean the number of calls made to leads with a specific lead score or the number of leads who entered a specific stage of the sales funnel owned by the sales team.

- **Webinar outreach:** The number of emails sent or calls made to leads who have signed up for a webinar, attended a webinar or not attended a webinar.

- **Magnet outreach:** The number of emails sent or calls made to leads who have signed up for a magnet, engaged with a magnet or not engaged with a magnet.

- **Form submission responses:** Number of sales team responses to submitted forms. Measurements can include emails sent, calls made, chat sessions or in-person sales calls. The number of responses should be equal to or great than the number of form submissions you have received.

- **Response time:** Response time to inquiries or form submission. This KPI could be response time for chat interactions, email inquiries, inbound calls, appointment requests or form submissions. Remember, time kills deals, so creating response rate goals for any lead-to-sales interaction points improves your overall sales success.

SALES POPULATIONS

There is tremendous value in understanding the existing populations and their rates of change within each stage of your sales funnel. These

KPIs indicate success or friction points in the sales process, can help the integrated team find quick wins and help them determine an estimated dollar value of leads within the sales funnel. You are looking for population totals and changes that can be directly attributed to sales activities. The most common sales populations KPIs are the following.

- **Population of sales-ready leads:** The number of leads sales owns, often measured over set periods of time to understand the number of new leads and leads being successfully cultivated by the sales team.

- **Population of first appointments:** The number of leads who are currently scheduled for initial appointments with a member of the sales team. This is especially relevant if marketing generates the appointments for sales.

- **Population of follow-up appointments:** The number of leads who are currently scheduled for follow-up appointments.

- **Population of deals or opportunities:** The number of potential sales, filtered by the number of potential sales in the different stages of the sales process. For example, you may have one hundred potential sales with fifty leads who are awaiting proposals, thirty leads considering proposals and twenty leads who are currently negotiating a sale.

- **Population of deals won and deals lost:** The number of sales that have been successful or have fallen through.

Sales and Marketing Scorecards and Accountability

Many companies set up scorecards and track KPIs without making people responsible for the results. This is a mistake and a critical area for sales and marketing alignment. Team members from both the sales and marketing teams must hold accountability for each metric and every KPI in the scorecard. Until your sales and marketing organization documents who is accountable for each stage of the integrated funnel, you won't be able to distinguish between successful campaigns and tactics that fall flat.

Integrated sales and marketing teams must review these responsibilities and KPIs as well as collaborate to fine-tune messaging and content to fit lead and customer needs. Leadership backing will make the development of a data-driven, data-led culture much easier and are key to making these assignments.

As the teams become integrated, you will find great insights from many team members on how they can best take ownership for KPIs and maximize results from the integrated funnel.

The Sales Placemat and the Integrated Scorecard

So far, we have discussed using the Sales Placemat, which was introduced in chapter eleven, to plan sales milestones, touchpoints and automations at every stage of the sales funnel. We also discussed assigning accountability for tasks in each of the different stages of the funnel to members of your team. The third element of getting the greatest possible value from your Sales Placemat is using it to chart your KPIs and goals for each of those stages. Whoever owns that stage is responsible for collecting any predetermined KPIs and contributing them to the integrated sales and marketing scorecard. Do this for each stage of your funnel.

The KPIs That Should Be in Every Integrated Scorecard—And How to Use Them

In the prior section, we introduced different KPIs and how they can help teams evaluate the success of integrated sales and marketing efforts. This new section brings this thinking into a scorecard format that can create visibility, generate ideas and get integrated teams into action.

Three Things to Know Before You Look at Your Data

Before you look at your data, consider the three following points to help you interpret it in a way that is useful to your team.

YOU NEED TARGET VALUES FOR EVERY KPI

Target values contextualize the actual values of your KPIs and are traditionally measured weekly, monthly and quarterly. Many of these values will be best guesses until you have enough data to set a reasonable baseline. From this baseline, you can start to make clearer forecasts and even set new and higher performance goals.

For example, if you have a specific target value for the number of appointments you want to generate each month, use this as the value that you measure the number of actual appointments against. If you say, "We scheduled ninety appointments this month," it is hard to say whether that is a major success or falls short. If you say, "We scheduled ninety appointments with a target of one hundred," it is much easier to tell how much further you need to go.

FOCUS ON PERCENTAGE CHANGES

Numbers like your total lead population or the number of proposals you have outstanding give you a general sense of quantity or scale, but without an understanding of how those values change over time, you won't understand the significance. Look for percentage changes, not just the absolute values of populations. This focus on the change in percentage will provide your team with more insight into whether you are gaining or losing ground and the magnitude of those changes.

FILTERED OR SEGMENTED DATA REVEALS MORE

As you get more and more proficient at gathering data and calculating KPIs, you benefit more from filtering or segmenting it. These filters or segments can be organized by performance, by campaign or tactic, by offerings or by salesperson.

If you don't filter your data, it will hide important details from you. For example, you may have an overall close rate of 35 percent of every proposal, but if you look further, you may find that you have a salesperson with a 45 percent close rate and others with 25 percent close rates. Being able to filter your data provides more insights that can be used to improve overall performance. We dive deeper into interpreting your data in the next chapter.

High-Level Performance KPIs

Our recommendation is to always lead with these KPIs, as they are closest to revenue. Staying focused on the value of your sales pipeline provides important visibility into the overall health of the organization. These are the KPIs that give you a quick glance of the overall revenue health. We recommend organizing these KPIs into two groups, new customer revenue and repeat customer revenue. These values are typically tracked weekly, monthly and quarterly.

- **Revenue:** Total sales related to new customers; this can be further segmented by offering.

- **Close rate:** Close rates related to new customers; this can be further segmented by offering.

- **Forecasted revenue:** Estimated value of new customer sale funnel; this can be further segmented by sales funnel stage.

Marketing Performance KPIs

These KPIs show how effective your marketing efforts are at generating new leads for sales. We recommend you look at them in relation to specific campaigns whenever possible. However, looking at these KPIs as a whole is also worthwhile since much of the success of marketing involves surrounding the lead with your company's content via multiple channels (reviews, social media, website and blogs, newsletters, etc.).

Populations and Percentage Change

- Website and blog traffic

- Sales funnel stages

- Newsletter sign-ups

- Magnet downloads

- Appointments generated

Campaign Performance Values

- Total leads generated

- Cost per lead

- Opportunities generated

- ROI

Sales Performance KPIs

These are the KPIs that are directly related to sales activities, their effectiveness and the dollar value associated with the current deals or opportunities in the sales funnel.

Populations and Percentage Change

- Aggregate opportunities or deals

- Total values for each opportunity or deal stage

Forecasted Revenue Values

- Aggregated opportunity or deal values (dollars)

- Total values for each opportunity or deal stage (dollars)

Evaluating Your Metrics as a Leadership Team

Without action, data is just numbers. The actions that sales and marketing teams take based on the data is driven by the team's leadership.

If sales and marketing are working together to bring leads into and through the funnel, they must join in conversation to prioritize activities and act on revenue growth or shortfalls. While each person on the sales and marketing team has their own set responsibilities and KPIs to track, the work of evaluating those KPIs and creating plans to strengthen weak points in the funnel starts with the leadership team. Scorecards should be reviewed in sales and marketing leadership meetings, following a specific agenda to be the most proactive.

Sample Leadership Meeting Agenda

This meeting agenda is structured so your sales and marketing leadership team can understand and optimize revenue between the two departments. This is for the department heads and their core teams to make sure they're moving toward revenue goals, identifying problems and using data to create strategies and actions.

What It Is: A data- and purpose-driven twice-monthly meeting that provides sales and marketing leadership insights into current revenue, short-term revenue forecasts and leading indicators associated with future financial projections.

Who Attends: Sales and marketing department head (or heads) along with their core or higher-ranking team members who are responsible for the KPIs (if needed).

Goal: Get ahead of problems and use data to create strategies and actions.

Use Case: Bring sales and marketing together to maintain and foster alignment, as well as ensure the two departments are being proactive to achieve revenue goals. The data in the meeting indicates whether the two teams should stay the course and work the current sales and marketing plan or get into action to pivot or generate new campaigns to achieve appointment and revenue generation goals.

Agenda: From the Bottom of the Sales Funnel Up

We recommend leading with KPIs closest to revenue, which most quickly impact sales performance. You can visualize this process as flipping your Sales Placemat upside down and starting with the data you have committed to tracking at the bottom of the funnel.

1. **Discuss sales: review bottom- and middle-of-sales-funnel KPIs and projections.**

   ☐ New revenue and repeat customer revenue

      • Current and forecasted revenue

      • Current and forecasted close rates

   ☐ Percentage population change for bottom and middle of the sales funnel

      • Aggregate opportunities or deals

      • Total values for each opportunity or deal stage

   ☐ Forecasted revenue values

      • Aggregated opportunity or deal values (dollars)

      • Total values for each opportunity or deal stage (dollars)

   ☐ Other KPIs: Close ratios, average sales cycle, join rates, no-shows, canceled appointments, percent collected

   ☐ Ideas/brainstorms for reaching sales and marketing target values if current values don't measure up

2. **Discuss marketing: review middle- and top-of-sales-funnel KPIs and projections.**

- ☐ Populations and percentage change

  - • Website and blog traffic

  - • Sales funnel stages

  - • Newsletter sign-ups

  - • Magnet downloads

  - • Appointments generated

- ☐ Campaign performance values

  - • Total leads generated

  - • Cost per lead

  - • Opportunities generated

  - • ROI

- ☐ Upcoming tactics with forecasted projections to goal

  - • Actual performance to forecasts and goals

    - ◦ New populations counts of sales funnel stages with increase or decrease in values, appointment performance per tactics

- Upcoming marketing initiatives and their impact on sales team

  ○ Ideas and brainstorms for reaching sales and marketing target values if current values don't measure up

3. **Discuss any next steps, owners, deliverables and mutually agreed-upon timelines.**

Data-driven marketing is a must-have for any organization with ambitious growth objectives. When you implement marketing scorecards, you empower your integrated team to continuously iterate and improve marketing campaigns in line with what your leads want and need. Marketing data and scorecards can help you understand your organization's reach while simultaneously enabling you to see what actions in the funnel are causing you to fall short of your projections. Through pressure testing, you can determine where your process needs to be tightened up, and your leaders can help guide the team to do the tightening.

Action Items

- Identify your sales and marketing data sources, which measure activity and engagement on your website, with your email and marketing automations and with your social media channels. Sources often include the social media platforms themselves, Google Search Console and your own marketing automation and CRM software. It is best if you use automation to flow this data into a single dashboard for easy collection and reference.

- Determine what KPIs you will use to measure the effectiveness of your marketing tactics both when drawing leads into the funnel and when moving them through the funnel from marketing to sales. These KPIs should help you evaluate whether your marketing tactics lead people to your website or landing page, whether those pages are getting engagement from leads, the perceived value of your offerings, the power of your CTAs and how your email marketing is moving leads through the funnel.

- Determine what KPIs you will use to measure how effective your sales tactics are, focusing on their efforts to follow up with leads and close deals. Consider both their sales activities and the populations within each stage of the sales process. Remember that the most useful way to evaluate populations is to focus on their rates of change rather than simply their absolute values.

- Set goals for each individual metric you want to measure and map these goals and metrics to each stage of the funnel using your Sales Placemat.

- Schedule a weekly or monthly digital sales and marketing leadership meeting to review your scorecards and KPI reports.

Chapter 16:
Risks, Successes and Reward Points in the Funnel

Use quantitative and qualitative data to identify where you can improve.

Now that you have a better understanding of the sales funnel, we take you deeper into its inner workings and teach you how to find opportunities for growth. We especially look at middle-of-funnel activities and how you can use data to keep leads from getting stuck.

"I don't know what we're doing, but it's working."

Often this sentence is said with pride after seeing a company's revenue trend up. However, it's a lot more insidious than one might think. That naïve positivity can lull people into a false sense of security, even as trouble prepares to pounce. If those in a sales and marketing organization don't know what they're doing right, they won't know what they're doing wrong when things start trending down.

They could be wasting too much money on ad spends to bring in leads when a different stage of the funnel needs to be improved. Maybe too much of the company's success is riding on one salesperson, who may one day decide to move on and take their profits with them. Without an understanding of where a company is succeeding and the data to back it up, no one will be equipped to fix problems when they do emerge.

Pull Your Sales Funnel Apart

We've made the case for the integrated funnel and why dividing it into stages matters. It allows sales and marketing teams to be efficient as they map tasks to the buyer's journey and improve performance.

Visualize your funnel with all your leads inside it. Now, imagine there are funnels for each of your ideal customers and their buyer's journeys nested inside of this greater funnel. If you want to be able to successfully optimize your sales activities, you must separate these funnels from one another.

For example, in Tom's business, there are two funnels: websites and digital marketing. Mostly there are two different sets of customers seeking out these services. It's true that the messaging surrounding his company and expertise should be consistent, but to sell most effectively, Tom needs to have different processes to meet these separate leads where they are and give them information relevant to the solution they are seeking. After all, someone who needs help with lead generation may not be interested in content about why mobile optimization is important, and someone who needs a functional website built from scratch may not be so interested in learning about Facebook ads.

The need for more than one funnel is not just about the content within it. It is also vital to track the KPIs from these different funnels separately so you can tell what effect they have on the amount of money you are bringing in. Otherwise, when you have a problem with revenue, you won't be able to tell where you need to bust out your magnifying glass and detect how to fix it.

How You Disguise Your Problems and Successes

The tendency to generalize leads causes sales and marketing professionals to overlook where they are winning and where they need to improve. There are three ways oversimplification creates risks of taking the wrong actions or even no action at all.

Risk Point One: Generalizing about Your Funnels

Let's say a teacher has a classroom of twenty students. Half of them are average students, about a third of them are high-scoring students and the remaining students are disruptive and get failing grades. It wouldn't be fair or accurate for the teacher to say, "All my students are problem students," even if that small group draws the most attention. Treating all the students the same wouldn't help any student in that class be successful.

The same goes for your sales and marketing campaigns. You could say, "All my efforts are useless," but if you haven't been tracking your data, you have no idea if that's true. In fact, the sales funnel for one of your offerings might have huge potential to draw more revenue even though the income from your other offerings has stalled. If you are looking at your results as a whole when you have multiple offerings, you can't see the specifics of what is and isn't working. You won't be able to see where you should keep doing what you have been doing or where you need to change direction.

Risk Point Two: Having Poor, Messy Data

Let's say a client has three offerings, but when they look at their revenue, they only look at the total rather than what comes in from each. Every month, when the client views their potential revenue and their deals, all they can see is whether the numbers are going up or down. Instead of asking why their deals aren't closing, they should have data that identifies how many deals they have for the first offer, how many for the second and how many for the third and how each of those funnels are performing. That allows them to diagnose the individual problems.

If you don't have your CRM set up to demonstrate these data points, the real statistics are hidden from you. Even if you have the knowledge that different offerings have different success rates, unless you are collecting data, you won't know how to act on that knowledge.

Risk Point Three: Generalizing about Your Salespeople

If looking at stats from all your sales funnels at once is unhelpful, lumping the performance of each of your salespeople together may be even more so. You might identify that your team has a 30 percent close rate, but you may have one salesperson with a close rate of 50 percent and another at 15 percent. The way you interact with these two different salespeople should not be identical if you want to make effective changes. Instead, the numbers should lead you to having personal interactions with the individuals on your team. Rather than give the sales team a blanket mandate to "sell more," it's more effective to take pointed action. That may mean focusing on helping the salesperson closing at 15 percent to improve, replacing them if necessary or supporting your top salesperson further until they reach superstar status.

There Is Gold in the Middle of the Funnel

What if there was another 10–20 percent worth of sales lingering somewhere inside your integrated funnel? If you are anything like many of our clients, there probably is. The good news is that we know you can find that hidden revenue if you look in the right place. By addressing spots where opportunities get stalled out—usually the tricky middle section where leads move from marketing to sales—sales and marketing teams can take action to get leads moving down the funnel again.

Leads often get stuck in the middle sales funnel as they continue to receive marketing content but don't take that crucial step forward to interact with sales. You can often recognize sticking points by looking for where leads are ballooning (Karl likes to visualize it as that cartoon of the boa constrictor with the suspicious lump in its midsection). If you see a place in the middle of your funnel where a disproportionate number of leads are gathering, that is a major indicator of where you are missing out on a sizable chunk of revenue.

Leads can stagnate for several reasons. It is easy for your progress to become buried mid funnel, and if you aren't paying attention, you might not even know gold is there. Perhaps a lead has finished receiving a marketing email sequence, but there is no next step for them to take that will put them in touch with one of your salespeople. Or maybe the leads are getting lots of information from marketing, but it isn't the information they need. **If you don't have your processes in place and mapped to the sales funnel, it can be frustrating to try to figure out which leads are ready to progress to the buying stage and which are still in need of nurturing. If everyone knows their role and you have complete data, you are much more likely to hit the mother lode.**

Here are a couple examples of how sales and marketing teams can cooperate to remobilize leads who become stuck in the middle of the funnel.

One of our clients noticed a few leads had been receiving and interacting with lots of marketing content but were not taking the next step to buy. The marketing team took the first step toward moving those leads forward by launching a "help us help you" campaign, where emails were sent to highly scored leads who were stalled. Those emails requested feedback regarding what sales and marketing were doing right or wrong. About one hundred people responded, allowing our client to adjust to the way they interacted with these leads.

Or sales can communicate with marketing to find out if there are highly scored leads sales can help target. Instead of leaving the marketing team to continue sending them content, salespeople could take it upon themselves to reach out in a person-to-person capacity. Leads can be mobilized by sales calling or sending personal emails inviting them to have a conversation.

Even people who engage with a company's marketing content on a regular basis and have high scores may need additional nurturing to progress beyond a sticking point. Some leads may be interested in a company's offering but still hang back from full engagement. Sometimes you just need to ask them to dance for them to finally decide to move forward from standing on the sidelines.

Finding and Fixing Funnel Clogs

The sales funnel has stages, touchpoints for digital marketing and steps for salespeople to follow as they nurture leads. When the activities and tracking metrics within these stages are set up correctly, you will be able to see where leads are getting stuck or having low conversion rates. You can also see where conversions are high and where you should be concentrating your efforts to replicate them.

Look for Larger and Growing Populations in Your Funnel

Identifying where populations are starting to balloon within your funnel is the first step to finding and clearing the clog. Usually, these leads are stuck somewhere in the middle stage, where they have for one reason or another not taken that next action to move them forward on their buyer's journey.

Use Quantitative and Qualitative Data for Insights

If you are scoring your leads and tracking them, you are more likely to be able to tell where their interest dries up. There should be an observable difference in the numbers between one action and the next. The numbers aren't going to tell you why people may be getting stuck or how you can fix it. Providing that qualitative data is where your integrated team comes in. If you can point out what activity is damming up the lead stream, they may be able to use their knowledge of the customers and the questions they ask and what they respond to and propose solutions.

Revisit the Steps You Take to Move Leads Down and Through Your Funnel

At Realtor Sales Skills, the integrated team leaders were getting better and better at looking at the qualitative and quantitative data in the sales funnel. In one meeting, Luke, the director of sales, brought the average attendance rate of the appointments that marketing set for the sales team to discuss. While the attendance rate had seemed to normalize around 75 percent, it still wasn't the result they were seeking. Luke asked Naomi, the director of marketing, what she thought they could do to increase the attendance rate. Naomi agreed to dig into the data and come back the following week with more insights and some recommendations.

What Naomi found was eye-opening. Appointments booked and held within seventy-two hours had an attendance rate of 85 percent, and appointments booked and held over seventy-two hours had an attendance rate closer to 60 percent. The data also showed that leads booked through the sales development representatives (SDRs) who called leads after webinars had almost a 100 percent attendance rate. Naomi brought this data to the next meeting with the recommendation to shorten the appointment booking window and have the sales development representatives call all the leads that booked more than seventy-two hours out to remind them of their appointment. Both tactics worked, and the attendance rate rose from an average of 75 percent to over 80 percent. Most months this translated to an additional eight to ten sales appointment attendees and three to four additional sales. Because the sales and marketing team had the data that showed when and where each lead booked their appointments, they were able to home in on the key issue that affected whether people attended the meetings they booked.

When you have the data attached to every activity in the funnel, you can see what next actions are not being taken, and you can investigate what might be keeping someone from taking it. If they sign up for your email list and then never open a single thing that comes into the inbox, you may need to review whether the content you are sending is valuable. If they are scheduling a meeting with a salesperson and then not showing up, it might be time to review the way you schedule meetings or send reminders. Discovering a solution to get leads flowing again might take some trial and error, but you will have the data to prove you are focusing on the correct problem rather than flailing around making uninformed guesses.

The Rewards of Targeting Your Choke Points

When you've tracked and quantified your problem areas, you will also get the satisfaction of seeing the numbers rise once one of your strategies begins to work. For example, the marketing department for one of our clients would organize twice-monthly webinars that generated about three hundred to five hundred sign-ups. However, only about 25 percent of people who signed up were attending. Marketing was doing their job by generating sign-ups, but they weren't sure how to change their technique to get people to actually attend the webinar.

This is where the magic of sales and marketing integration got to work. To fix this problem, we got the sales team involved and had them start calling people who signed up to remind them to attend. It worked.

Plus, there was another benefit to implementing this new strategy. It gave us a point to work from when we observed another chokepoint: people who attended the webinar but didn't book an appointment afterward. We tasked a sales development representative with contacting individuals who didn't book, and we were able to generate a 10–20 percent increase in appointments after each webinar. This went on to result in a 10–20 percent revenue boost as well.

If we hadn't had the CRM set up to track data for all our activities in the funnel, we would have been able to quantify only the very top and the very bottom. If marketing brought in a thousand leads and sales was only closing twenty of them, without data, the only suggestions would be for marketing to bring in two thousand leads or for the sales team to just try harder (whatever that means).

Make the Most of Your Sales Funnels

Every business leader wants to "do more of what's working and less of what's not." There are too many sales and marketing departments who don't know how to begin following that direction. Without clarity, you have no idea whether the actions you take to repair your revenue problems make any difference, positive or negative.

If you have one sales funnel set up for your company, you can have multiple. If you are tracking KPIs for the number of leads you bring in and the number of sales you close, you can also have them for every discrete activity in each of your funnels. Drilling down to those tiny details can help you diagnose problems and eventually multiply revenue.

Action Steps

- Create distinct sales funnels for each of your offerings.

- Set up your CRM to track data for individual activities in your funnel.

- Use quantitative data to identify where populations of leads in your funnel are bloating.

- Find your choke points and then bring your integrated team together to brainstorm how to get leads in these choke points to start taking the next action at a higher rate.

- Do more of what works and less of what doesn't.

Part Three:

Assembling and Mobilizing Your People

Chapter 17:
Banish Binary Thinking When It Comes to Your Sales Team

Balancing your team members' talents with your sales processes maximizes sales performance.

This chapter suggests that to nurture an effective sales team, you can't rely solely on a salesperson's winning personality or a detailed script for sales. You need to implement a complete palette of selling skills to maximize their performance.

Leaders seeking help often approach Karl with outdated ideas about how sales should be conducted based on specific salesperson archetypes. Take Cameron, for example, the CEO of an alarm system company that targeted commercial properties. In his conversation with Karl, Cameron expressed a common attitude that a single model of selling, and a single type of salesperson, holds the only path to success.

"Sometimes you just need to light a fire under them, tell them what to do and make sure they're doing it," he said. "Somebody needs to make sure they're visiting every commercial property in their territory, walking in and talking to the people in charge. And if they don't, we need to get them out of the company and off the team—simple as that."

In our experience, such a narrow approach doesn't work. Those people are going to be difficult to find, and the sales approach is going to be even more difficult to sustain. It also leaves no room for individual salespeople's unique talents and ways of selling to show themselves, let alone adaptations to the constantly changing business world.

One of the biggest mistakes sales and marketing leaders make is applying black-and-white thinking to the way they approach the behavior of their salespeople. Old-school attitudes about what a salesperson should do and how they should do it sets up leaders for disappointment and makes salespeople miserable. In this chapter, we explore two of these deeply ingrained, inaccurate beliefs. The first is that conducting sales according to a strict protocol is the only way to go. The second is that every successful salesperson has the same personality traits, usually geared toward being outgoing and dynamic, repeatedly bringing in more business with their charismatic techniques.

If there's one thing we want you to take away from this chapter, it is that people and their processes are not all the same—and that's a thing to embrace and capitalize on. This doesn't just refer to salespeople but also to the customers they serve. If you are too focused on following an inflexible sales process or making sure your salespeople all fit within a very specific mold, you'll be disappointed with the results.

The Importance of an Adaptive Sales Process

Here's a story to illustrate a situation where a rigid sales process stands in the way of good salesmanship. It starts with a forty-two-year-old woman walking into a car dealership and meeting a young salesperson who asks how he can help her.

"I'm here to buy an SUV," she says, unaware that the salesperson has just learned an exhaustive sales process that is about to affect the discussion.

Recently, the dealership invited a consultant to develop a protocol for selling to several ideal customer personas. Based on the personas they came up with, the consultant helped all the salespeople develop questions they could ask to get them closer to a sale. At first glance, our car salesperson has identified the person who has just entered the dealership as being close to one of the dealership's ideal customer personas: a fortysomething mother of three looking for an SUV to drive her kids to school and weekend soccer games.

"You can probably expect a mother to come in looking for an SUV to be able to bring the kids to school and sports practice and the like. Be ready to answer questions about practical issues like gas mileage and safety features," the consultant said.

With all that preparation, the salesperson is confident he can sell to the woman who just walked in. According to what he'd been taught, he starts the conversation with one of the questions on the dealership's "fortysomething mother of three" customer persona list.

"OK. How many kids do you have?" he asks.

"I don't have any kids," the customer says.

Right away, this customer has proven she doesn't precisely fit the persona our salesperson expected. However, he doesn't want to stray from the sales process everyone at the dealership agreed to. Unfortunately, he doesn't recognize the questions the consultant helped them develop as guidelines—he sees them as a hard and fast script to be followed at all costs. He decides to move forward with a series of questions about what the customer's typical day looks like, why she's looking for an SUV and what she wants to do with it.

"I'm just looking for a four-door Jeep Wrangler," she says. "I saw you have one on your website, and I want to test-drive it."

This customer has done her research already, viewing marketing materials that are available online. Through her own research, she has qualified herself into a lower stage of the sales funnel and is closer to buying. But our salesman has been trained to start working closer to the top of the sales funnel by getting to know the customer's current state and developing a more big-picture idea of what the customer is looking for in a vehicle. Instead of thinking of the process as nonlinear or noticing the possibility that customers could come into the funnel somewhere other than the top, he keeps plowing through his list of questions. With this approach wired into him by his superiors and the consultant, he soldiers on with his script and ignores her request to test drive the Jeep Wrangler.

"Do you care about gas mileage? Are there any other cars you're thinking about today?"

The customer feels alienated and a bit insulted at this point—like he isn't listening to what she wants and thinks he knows better. The salesperson thinks he's succeeding by following the sales process according to his training. To him, the script of questions is a way of showing the customer he cares about what she needs in a vehicle. However, he doesn't acknowledge how she is different from the persona or how she has done her research and already knows what she wants.

When we say your salespeople should build up processes to make sales to customers, we aren't talking about a rigid approach to every single lead. Inflexibility can result in the sort of problem we just described. It can make customers feel they are being judged and placed in a category rather than listened to as the unique individuals they are.

It is important for sales leaders to have processes mapped out for their people to refer to. However, no matter how well planned out your processes are, there is no substitute for listening and making a human connection. Leaders need to be sure they help salespeople develop their intuitive selling abilities so that they don't adhere so strongly to the process that they alienate customers.

The Myth of the Magical Salesperson

We've all seen this type of salesperson glamorized on TV and in the movies. They're aggressive but not too aggressive, assertive but not too assertive. They draw in new customers with little more than a sentence or two. They land enormous deals daily. The fact is, these salespeople are popular in movies and on TV because they are largely imaginary.

Some hiring managers daydream about finding a salesperson who knows how to sell to just about anyone. This mythical figure would be able to walk a customer through every step in the sales process, from catching their attention to closing the sale.

While holding on too tightly to a sales process can alienate potential customers, relying on personality can also cause major problems. Charismatic salespeople are rare and impossible to replicate. Additionally, they are more likely to move on to a job that offers them more money when the opportunity arises. Looking only for individual salespeople who can do it all is an unstable and unpredictable way of operating.

Instead of relying on a superstar salesperson to solve all your problems, consider all salespeople as part of a working whole. This means you must both understand the personalities who might come in for a job interview as well as what types of skill sets your business needs.

All Salespeople Are Not the Same

Sales leaders, including the alarm company CEO discussed at the top of the chapter, sometimes have the attitude of "You're a salesperson. Why don't you just get out there and sell?" They think salespeople should always be on the phone or introducing themselves to potential leads, chasing down new business at every opportunity.

But selling means a lot more than just going out and finding new leads (what does it mean to "just get out there and sell," anyway?). It can mean contacting a series of leads who provided their contact information at a tradeshow or networking event. It can also mean being diligent about following up with leads whom marketing has generated, answering their questions and meeting with them one or more times to close a sale. It can mean reaching out to current customers to introduce them to new offerings. Different salespeople excel at different techniques. It's up to a sales leader to uncover those differences in the members of their team.

Recognizing Your Team Members' Strengths and Personalities

One of Karl's clients employs a team of three salespeople who have all taken personality tests (DiSC) and sales assessments (Sales Achiever) to reveal their strengths and weaknesses, how they best learn and communicate, how they are motivated and how best to coach and manage them. However, their sales leader brought up to Karl that they weren't as successful as she wanted them to be.

"I keep thinking I need to find a way to make their lives easier," she said.

"Our job isn't to make a salesperson's lives easier," Karl said. "Our job is to figure out what they're really good at, make sure they're staying focused on it and get them the resources they need to be as effective as possible."

Karl suggested the leader ask each person on the team to come to their next one-on-one meeting with a list of ways they believed they should prioritize their focus and time. She would also ask them to have suggestions of how they could best use their own skills and traits to design the most optimal way for them to sell. The goal would be for the sales leader to align with the salesperson on what they should prioritize and learn more about their strengths, what resources they need and obstacles they need removed to reach their potential.

While you do want to help your salespeople grow, forcing them to lean into areas where they are weaker isn't the way to do it. That wastes time they could be spending using the strengths they already have. A sales and marketing leader's job isn't to teach people how to work harder at improving their weaker skill sets but to put people in roles where their existing skills can shine.

The Hunter and Farmer Framework (Proceed with Caution)

When you are determining someone's skill set, it helps to use a framework of hunter and farmer characteristics. Just like some people have a better head for numbers than others, or some may prefer sports to the arts, some salespeople tend to gravitate toward going out and seeking new business (hunters) while others would rather work to expand what they already have (farmers).

Keep in mind that these two different frameworks are just that— loose structures to help you evaluate and place team members where their talents are most needed. Much like the car salesperson in our earlier example should have been more sensitive to the customer's unique differences from the ideal customer persona, salespeople should not be treated as if they perfectly adhere to either the hunter or farmer profile. The following qualities are very general and don't substitute for complete personality assessments like Sales Achiever, CliftonStrengths or DiSC®.

THE HUNTER: A SALESPERSON FOCUSED ON FINDING NEW BUSINESS

Some salespeople have a lot of confidence and are enthusiastic about meeting new people and turning them into customers. When they dive into a networking event and give their business card to as many people as possible, they are demonstrating qualities of a hunter. They are more likely to thrive in business development than account management. Here are some other qualities that, if they are strongly present in a team member, put that person closer to the hunter end of the spectrum:

- On the high end of the assertiveness scale

- Happy to talk to strangers (e.g., meeting as many people as possible at a marketing event)

- Comfortable in situations others may view as uncomfortable (e.g., calling leads on the phone)

- Ready to take bigger risks in exchange for big rewards (agreeing to variations in income by choosing a high-percent commission for their salary)

- A thick skin and ability to take rejection in stride

THE FARMER: A SALESPERSON FOCUSED ON GROWING CURRENT ACCOUNTS

While salespeople with more hunter characteristics are excited by taking risks and meeting new people, salespeople who have farmer characteristics prefer more stability. Their qualities of being assertive and outgoing may score lower than someone who tends more toward the hunter profile, and they lean into growing relationships with people they already know and make great account managers. Here are some farmer characteristics.

- Care about harmony and building relationships more than competition

- Want to be seen as always adding value (e.g., they like to increase company revenue by growing accounts rather than finding new business)

- Get satisfaction from helping others (e.g., thrives on finding solutions to client's problems)

- Prefer stability in their job and relationships (e.g., more comfortable with a higher base income and low-to-no commissions)

Mapping Salespeople to a Personality Continuum

Instead of trying to decide whether a person is one or the other, envision a continuum of personality traits. On one side, you have a hunter, and on the other, you have a farmer. Any salesperson who is comfortable reaching out to new customers will be closer to the hunter end. Anyone who is more focused on cultivating relationships with interested leads is closer to the farmer side.

It's very unlikely any one person on your sales team will be all hunter or all farmer. In fact, to truly get a creative and diverse sales team, you wouldn't want a set of cookie-cutter qualities. Most people are a hybrid of both hunters and farmers, and either type is capable of closing business. Your job is to use assessments, communication and observation to determine where they fall on the hunter-farmer spectrum and, as a result, the best way for them to bring the most value to your organization.

Once you analyze whether people on your team are already doing tasks that use their unique talents or whether they need to have different assignments, it's time to develop winning processes that mesh their unique personalities with the responsibilities they hold.

How Flexibility Helps Salespeople Thrive

Amy from United Events, whom we first met in chapter twelve, is a successful salesperson with a nice book of business and a system that works to generate new leads and generate sales. She divides her leads into two categories: one full of people she already knows and one full of people she doesn't know yet. She creates two different sets of email templates to align with each of those two categories. With the former, her writing voice is more familiar, and her content focuses on reengaging people based on their past relationships. With the latter she still has a series of email templates, which she approaches with a more formal tone.

Amy is a hybrid hunter/farmer, but she is mostly a farmer. She has developed as a salesperson based on the areas where she excels: writing emails and cultivating relationships. She has been willing to commit to contacting new leads via email and LinkedIn and leaving after-hours voice mails for leads she thinks are an especially good fit. However, if Amy were asked to start making cold calls to these leads during the workday versus her routine of emails, LinkedIn and voice mails, she would probably leave her job (or at least spend her days a nervous wreck) and the company would miss out on the business that she is great at cultivating.

People in leadership positions often do not understand these different methods of operating. Their understanding can be as simple as

"Salespeople are there to get on the phone and make calls until they close business." There is a tendency to assume that every salesperson is assertive and outgoing and that they mostly have the personality of a hunter. Seeing salespeople in this narrow way misses out on an entire continuum of personalities and talents who can build processes and score wins for themselves and the companies they work for. If a new sales manager came in and demanded Amy start making cold calls to generate leads, the new sales manager would lose a solid salesperson with a system that works for her and the company.

We've said it before, and we'll say it again: your salespeople are not robots. Rather than try to program them to follow a specific set of rules and tasks in a particular order, let them get the work done in a way that works for them. Process does not supersede personality, and that's true the other way around as well. The two qualities need to sit on the same plane when it comes to your sales and marketing team's structure and the way they do their jobs.

Action Items

- Scan your team members to see if each salesperson is in the right role. For example, are you asking a salesperson who engages in more farmer activities to play the role of a business development person who does outreach and attends events? Or are you asking a hunter who wants to get out and meet new people and create new relationships to manage and service house accounts?

- Ask a series of guiding questions to help team members recognize their own strengths, look for activities or roles that best align to who they are and then set goals that leverage these skills.

- Evaluate your sales processes and any sales activities you think every salesperson needs to complete and determine if they are too rigid to truly set each person up for success. Consider adapting or evolving any defined processes to have more flexibility and aim to manage by outcome instead of activities.

Chapter 18:
Becoming the Coach of a Winning Team

Understanding the human side of sales and marketing alignment makes your team more than the sum of its parts.

In this chapter, we explore what you can do as a team leader to identify, avoid and correct trouble in your sales and marketing organization. You learn how to provide an environment that invites feedback and builds trust, as well as how to motivate team members to succeed and commit to common goals.

Many people view teamwork from a passive perspective. They believe it is simply something your company has or does not have. If you have a group of salespeople who are good at closing business and a group of marketers who bring in leads, then the team gets along and they don't really need a lot of team building. Basically, they're a "team," and they're "working" just fine.

The true definition of *teamwork* is not static and passive; it is dynamic and ongoing. Our goal in this chapter is to help you reprogram your understanding of the word *team* to the point it moves from passive to active.

Effective teamwork consists of individuals who bring their collective strengths and skills to your company. Together they empower one another to grow their individual skills and use them to excel in their roles. When your culture, company leadership and team members are all focused on each other's success, *team* becomes a verb and not a noun (this is why we call it *teaming* when using it in practice). Teamwork can be defined as a group acting together to create better outputs than what each person could do individually.

To maintain this ideal state, leaders must hold the space for teams to come together, listen to the advice of professionals and commit to encouraging growth for the team as a whole and for each of its members. Most employees want this—to put their skills to their highest and best use, be appreciated for their contributions and use their strengths to improve both their own and the company's realities. People want teamwork and thrive when it works well.

Clues Your Teaming Needs Help

When things aren't right with individuals and teams, you can typically feel it, see it and hear it. The team is sluggish, detached or edgy. People show up to work or meetings late and come across as disengaged. Your more vocal employees may even tell you directly or you may pick up on negative attitudes when you overhear sidebar meetings. In the world of sales, signs like these spell trouble. There are some universal truths when it comes to root causes of a frustrated sales team. Three of the most common are:

- Revenue is down and the sales team believes there is nothing they can do to improve it. In these cases, they often feel like victims or like success is out of their control.

- There are changes the teams don't like or agree with. These are often new policies or shifts in how your offering is marketed, sold or delivered. Salespeople believe these changes are making the sales funnel less effective, decreasing sales performance and impacting their commissions.

- Directions from leadership are misaligned with what the sales team believes they can control or impact, or they are inaccurate or based in a different reality than the sales team lives in.

Marketing teams can experience similar feelings based on other sources of frustration. Three of the most common are:

- They feel leadership or the sales team blame them for lower revenue performance, believe they are not doing enough to get results or think they "don't get" how high the stakes are for the sales team.

- Lead generation or marketing performance gets derailed by things out of their control, like mistakes made by their digital agency or global changes from Google or Facebook.

- Leadership overstep and seek results too quickly or tie results to things marketing cannot control (like revenue).

There are also shared scenarios that negatively affect both departments:

- Frequent or long meetings that keep the team from getting into action and where their presence is low or no value. Since sales-people have a finite amount of time to make calls every day, meetings during peak sales hours jeopardize their ability to do their job.

- Having the sales or marketing team do administrative tasks that are not the highest and best uses of their time (e.g., asking the marketing or sales team to fulfill promotional materials or pack and ship products).

- Having leaders micromanage individuals and the team. Examples include reading their email correspondence or tickets in platforms like ZenDesk or second-guessing the team's actions while they are midway through a campaign.

Salespeople and marketing professionals are happiest when they are applying their skills to their highest and best use. Endless administrative tasks or low-value activities compete for time and energy with your salespeople's revenue-producing activities and marketing team's execution of strategies and tactics. If lots of their income come from commissions, the sales team may become especially frustrated, because their income is directly affected. Drowning a team in busywork will jeopardize revenue performance, demotivate your teams and cause them to become increasingly dissatisfied with their jobs.

Co-Creating Solutions Is Better Than Dictating Directions

Many leaders think teamwork is dependent on how well a team can execute tasks that come from the top down. The leaders who make these top-down decrees are most likely to think this way. From their point of view, the sales and marketing team is just there to take on whatever job their manager tells them to without question. Approaching business in this way prevents the integrated team from making sales and marketing magic. **Instead, if we allow people in sales and marketing to get to know each other, understand their roles and strengths and solve problems together, they will reach much better solutions than if someone at the top is micromanaging them and controlling all their tasks and activities.**

Not only do most challenges touch multiple stakeholders, but most solutions do as well. Co-creation is a process of coming together as a team to clearly identify a challenge and work together to build a solution. The team's power grows exponentially beyond what one person can do alone when they leverage the team's everyone's diverse skill sets. Getting everyone together to tackle challenges can generate a more complete solution around which everyone can agree. This decreases scope creep, miscommunication and the time it takes to get buy-in and train everyone.

Any stage or step within the sales funnel represents an ideal place for co-created solutions. A common example is in the middle of the sales funnel where responsibility for leads typically moves from marketing to sales. At this handoff point, both teams need to be in alignment to create the most effective transition.

An Example of Co-Creation in Action

At a SaaS company where Karl consults, there was a mishap where a live webinar crashed twice, kicking out all the attendees both times. The sales leader was livid since each webinar typically created $75,000 in new sales. The marketing leader was frustrated with the tech team for causing all of the marketing team's hard work to go down the drain. Emails were flying back and forth, and Slack channels were getting overrun with messages about what went wrong, how the issue would be fixed and who would fix it.

What happened next was genius and a perfect example of co-creation. The sales and marketing leaders told everyone to stop emailing and Slacking and then called an ad hoc meeting with only one ask: come to the meeting with a solution that would create value for the webinar attendees. When the meeting started, one by one each teammate shared an idea. By the end of the meeting, the team had taken bits and pieces of the different ideas and crafted a plan. All attendees would get an email with a link to a form to request a hard copy of the CEO's book, a link to the prior month's webinar recording and a call from a member of the sales team where the attendee would be thanked for their interest and offered the book as well.

The result of this experience was a solution that required both marketing and sales to come together and fulfill different roles to execute the plan. In the end, the webinar generated a similar amount of short-term revenue as it would had it not had technical difficulties. Even better, offering the book resulted in additional sales over time; what started as a disaster ended up generating even more revenue than expected. The mishap caused the team to come together and co-create a solution, and to this day it's provided the integrated sales and marketing team with a memorable win.

Regular Feedback Loops Help Integrated Teams Get Better

When people are working in the right places in the funnel and communicating within a team environment, it creates an active feedback loop. With that level of communication, defensiveness shrinks among your people and really great things happen. People are more likely to come together with solutions instead of accusations when problems arise, because everyone's input matters, and your organization benefits from a stronger culture, more visibility of data and faster decision cycles.

Sales and Marketing Is a Team Sport

More than any other part of business, the work done by sales and marketing teams is like a sports team that wins by coming together, playing their own roles, supporting others and having an intentional strategy for each game. There are wins and losses based on how well team members perform individually and how well they work together toward the same goal. Like with any winning team, the coach plays a significant role in success.

Earlier we talked about how the sales and marketing departments at Realtor Sales Skills responded to a low number of webinar attendees by bringing in an SDR to contact registrants ahead of the webinar.

Once the month's revenue numbers came in, it was clear not only that the SDR increased the number of attendees but that the number of attendees who scheduled appointments with the sales team and converted to sales had increased. In short, the plan definitely worked.

Sales and marketing leadership shared the good news with both teams and celebrated all the hard work of the integrated team and the effort put in by the SDR. The success of this newfound tactic proved that having the SDR call and personally inviting leads to the webinar was directly connected to more scheduled appointments and more revenue for Realtor Sales Skills. A few weeks after this sales tactic was successful, the cooperation of the integrated team and the ideas people brought to their integrated meetings accelerated and went further.

"That SDR solution for the webinar is doing pretty well," someone in marketing said during a joint coaching session run by Karl. "Did you know marketing is promoting two other on-demand webinars and a mini-class right now? We have one hundred people who signed up for each but hadn't even thought about calling them. Do you want to do it? Should we add this to the SDR's role?"

We knew this solution had worked in a very similar instance, and now there was an opportunity to replicate its success, brought to sales' attention by someone on the marketing team. Up until that point, sales didn't even realize those webinars were taking place, and this ended up being another area where there was gold to be found.

Because sales and marketing completed integrated meetings and were starting to see their shared success, there was room for new connections to be made. The integrated sales and marketing team knew they had the shared space and environment to make these connections and be successful because of the cooperation between the teams. Reviewing sales funnels for individual campaigns, and who passes the baton to whom, makes these things into relay races instead of marathons, where everyone gives their all and depends on their teammates to give their all to bring them across the finish line.

Because your teammates identify and complement your highest and best use, teaming makes everyone greater than the sum of their parts. More than that, if your sales and marketing teams can do the same thing with one another, they're going to multiply one another's value to make your company successful. In the case of Realtor Sales Skills, it was unsurprising that adding the SDR to the other campaigns created additional revenue as well.

Bringing out the Best in Individuals Brings out the Best in Teams

When your team feels understood, supported and empowered, their individual and collective performances increase. When this happens, it's amazing to observe and be part of. However, like everything else involved in running an aligned and integrated sales and marketing organization, this comes from intentionality and setting up the entire team to win.

It starts with understanding that your team is made up of people who all have their own individual personalities. It's a simple concept but one that is often overlooked. People do best when they feel valued, are able to play to their strengths and are supported.

To give valuable feedback to one another, team members must be aware of each other's strengths and the places where they might need more support. Once you've evaluated your team member's personalities, strengths and the tasks they can best master with those strengths, you can help them to help themselves. Karl often prescribes a series of questions that individual team members can use to evaluate their own performance and long-term and short-term goals. This Individual Performance Planner serves as both a self-discovery and a managerial tool, creating aha moments for the teammate and their manager and serving as a manual for how best to increase the happiness, effectiveness and performance of the individual. Some of its questions and reflective prompts include:

Strengths and Focus Areas

- What are your strengths?

- How could you use more of your strengths each day?

- What is your focus most days?

- What is your ideal focus each day?

- What might enable you to spend more time on your ideal focus areas?

Motivations and Motivators

- How do you describe motivators?

- What motivates you personally? Professionally?

- How do you feel when you achieve and/or experience your motivations?

- What do you wish you could do more of that would fill you up?

- What ideas do you have that would allow you to achieve more of what fills you up?

Goals—Personal and Professional

- What are your personal goals for the next ninety days and the next twelve months?

- What are your professional goals for the next ninety days and the next twelve months?

- What are the top three things you want to achieve in the next ninety days and the next twelve months?

Daily Activities and Priorities

- Write a list of the things you find yourself doing on a daily or near daily basis.

- Select which of those daily activities are low value or have low relevance to your job.

- Determine which are distractions from your job.

- List how many of the meetings you attend each week that are high value and aligned to your highest and best-use activities, versus those that are low value and not aligned.

- Consider how you can change your week to optimize your job performance and achieve your personal and professional goals.

Community Involvement, Networking and Education

- List organizations or associations you would want to be involved in and your desired level of involvement.

- List networking groups or networking opportunities you would want to be involved in and your desired level of involvement.

- List educational opportunities or skills you would want to learn.

- List how the organization could support you to achieve this involvement.

Note: There is a complete Individual Sales Planner template for an account executive in the appendix of this book. It includes additional questions more targeted to salespeople and explores sales targets, customer retention and growth and new account development.

Driving Sales through Team and Individual Incentives

Overseeing and running a sales team is a challenging and rewarding role. If you learn to turn all the right dials and integrate successfully with marketing, revenue performance drastically increases. A big part of driving this performance is about winning the hearts and minds of your sales team.

The historic model is that individual salespeople would be in competition with each other, working under the assumption that healthy competition drives everyone to perform. That is also no longer seen as a universal truth. **With all the resources and tools for collaboration, there is no reason to pit salespeople against each other as the sole path to driving overall sales. A blended approach rooted in getting to know what motivates each of your salespeople and incentivizing them accordingly is more effective.** It creates levers you can pull that incentivize each individual and the team in ways that drive the entire organization forward.

Motivation is never one size fits all. Not everybody wants to compete. Not everyone strives for individual accomplishments. If you think about your different salespeople and realize that each one of them is driven and inspired by different things, you can start to build incentives that match these different dimensions and characteristics. Some of them do like to compete against others, while others prefer to compete against themselves. Still others want the whole team to win together. You can set up monthly incentives for each of those scenarios. Ideas include:

Competition

- Highest overall sales

- Most units sold

- First to a certain number of sales

- Highest average sales price

Individual Performance

- Full pays versus financed sales transactions

- Sales targets by revenue or units sold

- Number of new appointments

Team Results

- Meeting a particular number of sales per month as a team. This one really drives teamwork and helps people want to work together and collaborate and help one another more; it brings out the best in people.

These different options give individual salespeople options for the type of incentives that make them feel good about what they are doing. Even better, group goals naturally lead to teaming as individuals encourage one another to do their best.

An empowering and supportive environment can turn a group of individuals doing individual work into a group of individuals working together. With mutual respect, co-creating processes and regular constructive feedback, your team members are more likely to learn by doing and leverage one another's strengths. The results will be evident from your sales team's attitudes and performance and, likely, your increased revenue.

Share and Celebrate Sales and Marketing Wins

With all the focus of working together, a big part of making these strategies stick is by sharing and celebrating sales and marketing wins. By now you're hopefully considering bringing your sales and marketing teams together on a regular basis to share insights and performance data, connect as a team and co-create solutions. We cannot encourage you enough to start doing this, but as you make these plans also consider how to set goals for the integrated team and celebrate wins.

On a basic level, we recommend starting a celebration gathering by asking each teammate to share a win and to acknowledge the actions of one of their teammates. If possible, we also recommend celebrating the achievement of monthly or quarterly goals associated with each stage of the sales funnel. The power of a simple "thank you" and clear recognition will strengthen your teaming culture and set the tone for a collaborative and impactful meeting.

Your celebrations don't need to be elaborate or expensive. This is about appreciation and creating a culture where individuals and teams are recognized for their hard work, alignment to company values and performance within their spheres of influence. Celebrations can include lunch, small bonuses like gift cards or even a revenue share associated with achievement of high-value revenue goals. The point is to bring people together, make goals visible and celebrate and reward both small and large wins.

Action Items

- Consider what it means to be the leader and coach of the sales and/or marketing organization. Are there additional skills you need? How do you want to be viewed? What type of impact do you want to have?

- Look for clues that will give you insights into whether your sales and marketing team might be frustrated or in need of your support.

- Explore whether your culture co-creates solutions or your team is simply being asked to implement directives. Determine which model you think will work best for your team, and if it's the co-creation model, start working toward this new paradigm.

- Implement integrated sales and marketing meetings (like those described in chapter fourteen) that allow your team to co-create sales processes and solutions rather than dictating the processes from leadership down.

- Review the Individual Performance Planner questions in this chapter and determine if they are something you want to implement with your team. If the answer is yes, consider using the template in the appendix of the book and meeting with each teammate in one-on-one meetings to work through the questions and get into conversations. To encourage sales, structure reward systems based on what motivates and empowers your team members the most, focusing on rewarding the group for successes achieved together.

- Start celebrating wins and making sure the integrated team is acknowledged and thanked for their hard work, effort and success.

Chapter 19:
Building a Well-Rounded Marketing Team

Cultivate the roles and skills of each marketing team member to align with the sales team.

This chapter reviews the eight key marketing functions needed for your company to build awareness and generate leads along with which of those positions should be outsourced and which can be cultivated internally.

Several processes in the sales and marketing funnel are managed by the marketing team. Understanding what those roles are, their places in the funnel and how they interact with one another help ensure a complete and integrated sales and marketing funnel. This also determines the points of connection between sales and marketing and who on the marketing team keeps lines of communication open. Remember, each part of the funnel is enhanced when the work of the marketing team is informed by the sales team's findings.

These marketing positions are focused on generating top-of-funnel awareness and mid-funnel inquiries. Once you have a clear idea of what is needed in each part of the funnel, you can identify where collaboration is possible and how both sales and marketing can come together to fill gaps in the funnel and move more buyers toward a sale.

The Eight Roles of a High-Performing Marketing Team

There must be people with a variety of skills to inform, plan and carry out the marketing tasks that keep your funnels moving. There should be people who are strategists, creative and cooperative content writers, eagle-eyed technologists, analytical researchers and persistent and communicative organizers and tacticians. We have drilled down the ideal set of essential marketing roles. Let's start by reviewing the roles most needed on your internal marketing team, and we begin with marketing leadership.

Marketing Leader

The marketing leader calls the shots and drives the strategy. It's amazing how many companies still wing it when it comes to this critical position. This leader is responsible for the overall execution of your company's marketing plan and accountable for the results. This position goes by various titles such as marketing director, marketing manager, chief marketing officer or VP of marketing. Depending on the number of people at the company and the number of hats each person wears, some people serve multiple roles, with marketing being one of them. The marketing leader could be the CEO or someone doing double duty and leading the sales team as well.

We often see the duties assigned to a marketing leader spread across different members of the company. This can cause delays and confusion. While collaboration is something we strongly encourage, strategic marketing decisions by committee are not. **The marketing leader should have final approval or veto power in the areas that follow and drive the company's overall marketing strategy and direction.**

The marketing leader is responsible for the direction of the marketing team. They are the key point person when it comes to all things marketing related, which means they are also the point person for aligning with the sales team. They must keep the doors open and continuously invite the sales team to discuss upcoming campaigns and initiatives. If there is a separate person leading the sales team (and they are not responsible for both), they need to be in constant communication with them so that no valuable information falls through the cracks. Responsibilities of the marketing leader include:

- Getting into a conversation with the sales leader to decide on a course of action for sales funnel strategy

- Approving content, website launches and visual branding

- Reviewing and approving key messaging

- Leading the strategic marketing meetings and bringing in sales team members to get their input and qualitative data

- Reviewing and evaluating marketing metrics side by side with the person leading sales, viewing it in context of integrated sales and marketing funnels

Project Manager or Coordinator

It's essential to have an effective, organized person to juggle all the details of sales and marketing initiatives. Without a project manager or coordinator who knows how to manage multiple responsibilities, action items and deadlines, sales and marketing integration and alignment are in danger. This person is responsible for scheduling and setting milestones, building accountability for sales and marketing tasks and assignments and making sure everyone has what they need to move forward. They are often forgotten when things go well but blamed when things go wrong. It's a challenging job and critical for success in sales and marketing alignment. Project manager or coordinator responsibilities include:

- Scheduling and organizing the strategic digital marketing meetings

- Organizing and following up on action plans

- Managing communication between the strategic digital marketing team members

- Updating online project management software for improved team coordination

- Looking for inconsistencies in team member action items

- Checking the website for broken links and other errors

- Preparing due dates for action items and assigning responsible people

- Helping recruit and replace team members as needed

- Communicating with contracted team members and other subcontractors

- Organizing website content timing and placement on the website and in social media

- Supporting key sales and marketing leadership positions

Digital Marketing Specialist—Top of the Funnel

This is an important tactical position, responsible for activities that bring people into the top of the integrated funnel. They are responsible for driving traffic to a company's website, getting exposure in social media and other tactics that make people aware of the company.

It is vital the content used to drive growth in the top of the funnel is consistent with the integrated sales and marketing team content recommendations. This role determines how to best use that content to drive brand awareness. This position requires content skills, social media expertise, SEO knowledge, Google Ads experience and other top-of-funnel skills. The digital marketing specialist's responsibilities include:

- Preparing and implementing a top-of-funnel traffic generation plan for the website and social media

- Conducting keyword research and developing keyword themes for SEO, using messaging and content agreed upon by the integrated sales and marketing team

- Reviewing website content and providing SEO content for the website code and on page content

- Setting up, managing and reviewing Google Ads and all online advertising programs

- Overseeing and setting up social media efforts for consistent design, content postings and distribution through targeted social media outlets

- Working with content writers on regular blog posting topics and SEO coding for all blog posts and other website content pages

- Coordinating top-of-funnel efforts to direct leads into the appropriate sales funnels according to parameters established by the sales and marketing team (based on lead source, categorization, etc.)

- Setting up, collecting, analyzing and reporting website traffic sources as seen in web stats

Funnel Manager—Digital Marketing

When it comes to integrating the sales and marketing teams, this position is one of the most important. The funnel manager is responsible for making sure leads keep moving through the funnel from the time they enter, through the middle to the point where they make contact with a salesperson. They manage marketing automation with HubSpot, Marketo, SalesForce and other apps. The touchpoints and activities listed and described in chapter twelve are all managed by this person, mostly through marketing automation software and email marketing. They collect data about what leads are responding to within the funnel, then analyze and present it to the integrated team. They should have some psychology and communication skills mixed in with a sharp eye for data interpretation. It is also important that this person be able to make recommendations based on these findings; their reports are the starting place for whatever the rest of the team decides to do. They are tasked with:

- Reviewing web stats weekly or monthly, comparing them against previous months/years and spotting trends in the data and then making recommendations

- Managing the monthly email newsletter and other email marketing efforts

- Developing and executing on marketing automation programs and the overall marketing dashboard

- Developing user testing programs to gather feedback from website users

- Communicating with sales and marketing team members about how best to score leads and then implementing those methods throughout the marketing-led processes within the sales funnel

- Reviewing stats and data from email campaigns and other mid-funnel activities

- Developing reports for the integrated sales and marketing team and company leadership

- Setting up tracking for all relevant website conversion points

As your internal sales and marketing teams collaborate to carefully build funnels and craft messaging, it will often be necessary to bring in outside contractors, an agency and/or freelancers. If your internal team is conscientious and consistent about providing information to these support professionals, the benefits of their specialized skills will help your marketing stand out and get results. When you are looking for what should be outsourced, start with specialized skills not found on your team nor likely to be needed in a full-time position.

The following roles must be filled with people who are experts, not jack-of-all-trades freelancers or random team members.

Digital Content Writer

Businesses frequently use contracted writers for website content or email marketing content. Many companies lack qualified writers on their team, and this is normal. Most people hate to write—they hated to write when they were in school, and they don't like to write at their job. The good news is there is no shortage of excellent writers who can write about your industry for your target market better than anyone else on your team. These writers are an essential part of your sales and marketing efforts.

Writing high-quality marketing content is a skill and a specialty worth investing in. For the investment to pay off, marketing leaders must be aware of the collaboration that takes place between sales and marketing and the resulting messaging strategy. Your content writers must hear from both sales and marketing teams.

One of the most awkward things that can happen during a sales call is for a prospective buyer to point out problems with the content they are reading about your company. A common refrain is "What you are telling me on this call is not what I read on your website."

This is solved through excellent communication between the sales team and the marketing content writers. It is important enough that the marketing funnel manager or marketing leader should take responsibility for connecting the sales team members with the content writer.

Content writers will need a lot information about the company. It's a good idea to share your marketing plan and strategy with them. Writers will also need to know about keyword research findings for SEO, detailed service and product information, procedural information about how leads move from one step in the funnel to the next, information about current promotions and campaigns and other factors that move buyers into action. The content writer is responsible for the following:

- Meeting with the strategic digital marketing team to devise a content plan that includes content topics, distribution channels and a schedule for generating written content

- Recommending content approaches for length of content and use of headers by content type

- Writing blog posts, marketing emails, website content, social media long-form posts

- Consulting with members of the sales team to ensure content accuracy and get new ideas for content based on their qualitative data

- Reviewing web stats on the most popular content and how it is being read by website visitors and recommends new content topics

- Ensuring all written content is in a format easily read and understood by online visitors

- Understanding the goals of each piece of content and preparing content that meets those goals, such as improved SEO, conversion, general information and more

One final word on content writers: It often takes two to three attempts before writers can find your company's voice and write marketing copy that gets results. Review a few drafts before you make the final call on which writer to hire.

Multimedia Provider—Photography, Video and Audio

Marketing leaders and project managers are also responsible for coordinating the efforts of multimedia providers. These providers create audio, video and photographic content according to the direction provided by sales and marketing. Again, these contractors specialize in these skills and will get you much better results than if you were to just send anyone on your team out to shoot video or take photos. Impressive images on your website will appeal to users right away.

Photography is the most common type, but video and audio also provide variety and points of interest. As with the writer and other contract positions, the multimedia provider needs to have an open line of communication with the marketing leader along with input and thought leadership from the sales team. The multimedia provider's responsibilities include:

- Preparing photoshoots, capturing the photos and editing them for online placement

- Preparing the storyboard and script for video production work

- Shooting, sound mixing and editing online videos

- Recording and editing audio recordings, such as podcasts, music and other audio clips

- Working with the graphic designer on layout and placement of all media elements

- Ensuring all media is easy to use on the website and provides value to visitors

- Understanding where the best platform for each type of media, whether that be on a website or on social media

Video content has become a critical part of the integrated sales funnel. Keep in mind, most people do not watch videos on websites; they watch videos on YouTube and other social media sites. Also, avoid stock photos where you can. The best photography is always of your team, clients and stakeholders. Use captions on your photos so people know who is in the photo and their roles at your company. Photos are the most highly viewed element on a website. Make your photos worth the time of your website visitor.

Graphic Designer

Graphic designers are responsible for the look and feel of your brand. They create and design websites and all marketing collateral. They develop brand colors, logo and all the necessary design elements.

Graphic designers must design for your target marketing, not individuals on the marketing team or for the designer themselves. They must also have a good sense for usability and how people engage with digital designs, like websites and apps. The graphic designer's responsibilities include:

- Preparing the website home page design and interior page designs

- Updating the home page banner and other graphics as needed

- Integrating the website's messaging and taglines into the graphics of the website

- Ensuring all photos, videos and other graphic elements are a consistent part of the overall brand

- Working with the technology team so all design and graphic elements are properly coded for SEO purposes

- Providing design elements for all social media sites and other online graphics

Technology Professional

Technology is a critical part of sales and marketing. Without excellent website hosting and a website that fires on all cylinders, loads fast and meets user needs, the integrated sales funnel is in trouble. A trained and knowledgeable IT professional must be available to help with tech-specific issues like website coding structure, hosting, e-commerce and other programming and development needs for the website.

They need to be available for support; if the technology falls apart, it can result in lots of lost opportunities and major frustration for the team. You want a well-rounded technology expert who can do development tasks in addition to troubleshooting problems. Specifically, we recommend this person be well-acquainted with the WordPress platform, which is the most popular website CMS platform as of the writing of this book. Your technology professional is responsible for the following:

- Selecting the appropriate website platform that meets the needs of the website strategic plan and can also be edited by internal team members

- Establishing the hosting environment for the website, along with email accounts

- Setting up access to the website's administrative sections with passwords and training for making website edits and updates

- Establishing and overseeing the security functions for the website and other spam and malware protections, along with the domain name hosting and DNS configuration

- Overseeing the integration of the website with any company software modules such as accounting systems, CRM software, inventory or other types of software

- Using or customizing the functionality within your tech stack and aligning this technology to the needs of the sales and marketing teams

Moving Roles from the Outside In

Skilled consultants no doubt play an important role in sales and marketing alignment. As you build a team to reach your sales goals, there will be a mix of internal and external team members. External teams can fill in several valuable gaps on your current team. Ultimately, it's ideal to have people on your internal team who have the skills to fulfill the tasks needed for the four internal roles just described. However, it can also be useful to start by outsourcing at first and then handing off responsibilities to internal staff once ready.

This can be an especially good call when your leadership team is uncertain about how to compile a balanced team. Remember that you can hire consultants and agencies to help with your hiring and training process as well. They could be useful in helping select the right contractor or marketing agency to help you get started and could also provide the training you need to be self-sufficient with your marketing strategy and execution.

Hiring an Effective, Well-Rounded Marketing Team

All eight roles must be filled adequately to get marketing results. Be mindful as you evaluate your current team and determine which team member skills are best suited for each role. Be careful of people wearing multiple hats. For example, it is nearly impossible to find one person who can both generate creative content and evaluate KPIs, or who can both coordinate your projects and do SEO or who can both shoot video and drive traffic.

Use the roles in this chapter to put people in the right seats. Fill in the gaps by hiring new team members, using outside help or rounding out your existing team members' skills with training.

Action Items

- Appoint one person to be the decision-maker for marketing, to have the final word on campaigns and overall strategy. Making decisions via committee can waste a lot of time and is not recommended.

- Identify who is the digital marketing specialist, responsible for top-of-funnel marketing activities, versus the funnel manager, who is responsible for activities taking place between the top of the funnel and where a lead moves on to interact with the sales team.

- Hire a funnel manager and make this person responsible for establishing and managing marketing automation workflows.

- Alert internal marketing team members what their responsibilities are when it comes to working with outside contractors, who will be setting up those contractors with the information they need and the contacts within the sales department who can help them create useful content.

- Be sure whatever content writer you use has contact with the sales team to ensure they are providing accurate insights and messaging, and make sure your sales team reviews the content that does get posted on your website or sent out as part of your email marketing.

- If you are missing any of the listed skills and responsibilities, determine whether you should outsource, hire new team members or train any of your existing team members in those areas. Assign contractors, recruit an agency or hire freelancers to fill in the gaps on your team.

Chapter 20:
Hiring an Effective Sales Team

The way you hire sets up your sales and marketing organization for success.

This chapter helps you evaluate what type of salespeople best fit your business needs, the scenarios where you need the extra sales support (or leadership) and what you should have prepared before someone joins your team.

You know by now how important your people are to your business's success. Even the most carefully planned strategies and processes go wrong if you don't have people who are ready to apply their talents to teaming skills. At the same time, you need to know how you want your salespeople to sell for you before they come on board.

Hiring for marketing positions in a digital world is a lot more likely to be seen as people fulfilling concrete functions (e.g., analyzing data, creating digital marketing campaigns or writing website content). Hiring salespeople may seem to call for more intuition, but that doesn't mean you should hire now and work out the details later—quite the opposite. Your sales team members fulfill roles and responsibilities in the sales funnel, and you need to make sure that their skills and personalities match up with what your business needs.

Five Sales Team Growth Challenges

When companies need to build or restructure a sales team, it often takes place during an exciting period of growth. That is likely the time when you'll feel the most urgency to get some superstar salespeople on your team; however, hiring new salespeople is a process that should be addressed with caution to avoid risks to your bottom line. See if you recognize your company in any of the following business scenarios.

Scenario One: Growing Beyond Word of Mouth and Hiring Your First Salesperson

Trevor had just been appointed VP of his dad's landscaping supply company. This was a years-old mom-and-pop operation built on Trevor's dad's reputation and individual customer relationships. Now they wanted, and needed, to grow beyond word-of-mouth and one-on-one connections. That was not going to happen unless Trevor got smart about hiring a sales team and intentional about finding new customers. Trevor had no idea where to start. With an urgent need for something the company had never had before, there were many ways this scenario could go wrong. How could Trevor avoid making mistakes when building a sales team for the first time ever?

Scenario Two: Trying to Clone Yourself to Grow Faster

In many cases, the founder of the company is the only real rainmaker and is responsible for all the company's revenue growth. Benjamin, founder and CEO of MaxDevPartners, who we referenced in chapter seven, knew his business inside and out, but he had never laid out processes for other salespeople to follow. Whenever MaxDevPartners was in touch with a new prospect, everyone knew that Benjamin had to be on the sales call for it to go well.

CEOs in a scenario like Benjamin's know that if they want to grow faster, they need to hire someone to find and grow new deals. They hit a capacity limit and get frustrated and burnt out. "If only I could find someone who sells exactly like me, then we could grow this business faster," they think. They are more likely to then hire based on who they think may be a superstar, either someone who makes the top sales numbers at a competitor or someone they meet while out networking who complements their own personality. However, every salesperson is different, and trying to duplicate oneself can lead to micromanaging and frustration for both the salesperson and the owner when they don't have the knowledge, authority or connections to replicate the founder's sales abilities. When companies hire salespeople this way, they are taking a major gamble limiting their chance of success. They may also feed into anxieties and false beliefs within the company that only the owner can close sales.

Scenario Three: Scaling Your Team by Adding More Salespeople

Going from one or two salespeople to a group of three to five can be tricky business. Sales organizations of this size often lack structure, processes and routines. Instead of operating as a team, each sales professional often does their own thing in their own way. While this can be effective in small, adaptive companies, it can create a false sense of scalability when it's time to add a few more salespeople to the organization.

Sarah runs a professional services company, where she and her two teammates generate all the sales. They were doing about $3 million in revenue, but partnering with a marketing agency increased the rate at which they brought in leads. Sarah began to eye a growth target of $5 million in revenue within the following eighteen months. To reach that goal, she hired two dedicated salespeople.

Though this was an exciting time, the opportunity to grow presented a new challenge—how would these new hires learn what they needed to do to live up to that opportunity? With no formal sales processes and no real sales leader in place, Sarah was concerned the new hires would not quickly adapt to the company or be able to communicate all the nuances of their offerings to leads. The challenge was to bring people onto the team and get them up to speed with how to communicate with and close business with the growing number of leads they'd been brought in to convert.

When a team reaches a point of needing to grow, but it's been selling with a more seat-of-the-pants approach, onboarding new team members the right way is invaluable. Being aware of the preparation needed to get someone acclimated to what the sales organization needs can help teams side-step the traps that can stop new hires (and their ability to sell) from meeting company goals.

Scenario Four: Finding Someone to Lead Your Sales Team

When companies want to level up their sales organizations, they may think that what they need is a capable new sales team leader. Not every company already has someone in place who can take the wheel, and hiring the right leader to support growth is tricky. Plenty of companies think the solution is promoting a superstar salesperson to a director or managerial role. This almost always poses more business risks than rewards, largely because being good at sales and good at management are two different skill sets. If you have someone who is good at sales placed in a role where they themselves are no longer selling, their talents aren't being used to their highest good. Better to find someone who understands sales organizations and how to uplift salespeople as they pursue their own and the company's goals.

When you seek out someone to lead your sales team, you must know what processes you have in place and what processes you need someone to help you develop. Some sales leaders could be considered "builders" and are good at building sales organizations from nothing. Others do much better as operators—managers who come in and competently run an existing machine. Even someone who would be a great manager could be set up to fail when expected to build a functional sales organization from the ground up. Be ready to ask questions to determine whether the leader you are interviewing has experience building systems and teams or mostly running and maintaining ones that are already in motion.

Scenario Five: Training Up a New Sales Leader

While taking your sales superstar and turning them into your sales manager is typically a huge mistake, there are times when someone from your sales team has the right mix of traits and interest to evolve into the leader of your sales department.

One of Karl's clients had a salesperson named Jeremy on their team who had solid sales but was also very dedicated and engaged when it came to teamwork. When Karl had a one-on-one and asked him about what his goals were for moving forward in his career, it was clear right away that he wasn't just focused on making more money. Jeremy had gravitated toward leadership ever since he had been the captain of a sports team in high school. He was enjoying his role as a salesperson, but he told Karl that when it came to his long-term career, he was hoping to find a role that allowed him to lead a team.

It just so happened the company was looking for a new sales leader for their organization. After his discussion with Jeremy, Karl recommended to the CEO that he be moved up to a sales leadership position in the company. With his institutional knowledge and his respected position within the sales team, he quickly and happily adapted to his position as sales leader. He was able to hit the ground running with existing team members and leadership structures and effectively train new salespeople in a player/coach model.

The model of promoting from within the company can work, and we have seen it work, if you have the right person. Here's some high-level advice: create a job description of the sales leader you want with a list of key skills and attributes. Then, score the salesperson you are considering against that list, create a gap analysis and create a road map with steps and milestones for the individual to achieve as they matriculate to this role over a set period of time.

Putting the Right People in the Driver's Seat

The point of investing in a salesperson is to increase revenue. It's not about spending money for the sake of it; most companies hope good teams lead to well-oiled revenue-growth machines. However, if you hire the wrong way, it can cost a lot of money for little return (other than a frustrated team). **Remember, you need two things: a plan to determine which people will be best at operating the machine and an instruction manual once you bring them on board.** You also need to know whether there is a machine there for them to operate at all or whether they will need to be part of engineering it.

Build a Sales Team the Right Way

If you see your company in any of the previous scenarios, you need to carefully consider your approach to hiring for your sales team. Making mistakes in how you hire (and prepare to hire) can carry a high risk of wasted time and money. Without a defined workflow or process for how your salesperson will find leads, communicate with them and close business, you can't trust your new hire will figure it out on their own. If you do hire people without giving them direction, your sales team members will feel unsupported and helpless, and those bad feelings could get worse over time. Here are things you need to think about as you build up an optimal sales team.

Step One: Set the Intention

Just like with anything else you want to build, you need to start with a plan. Recognize that you are seeking a more stable, scalable and replicable sales engine that will either take leads from marketing or generate leads itself, move these leads to opportunities, have professionals who will know how to close these opportunities or manage the team that will perform these tasks. Set the intention for a sales team and working funnel that can operate without a single person (in most cases the owner or founder) as the essential piece that makes everything go. Ideally, when the blueprints are laid out, you will recognize the pieces you need to keep it running on its own.

Step Two: Get Guidance

You'll need some level of guidance to get started whether or not you are already familiar with the ins and outs of sales and marketing. Learn about what it means to have a strong sales organization by reading books (like this one!), listening to webinars and talking to experts. In Trevor's case, he did a deep dive of his own into what a salesperson does, what tools they use and how they can come together to form a working department. His research made it clear that he was just one person, and he realized the only way to reach the growth goals he and his family wanted was to get some plans in place and then hire a well-rounded team of salespeople and marketers to execute it. He also knew there was an operational, process side that went beyond the individual people on the team.

Step Three: Set Up Your Salespeople

Too many people think that they can hire a salesperson, park them in front of a phone and then say, "OK, get selling!" Making sure they're set up with the tools, resources and objectives they need is essential. Figure out answers to these questions before you even begin to try and hire someone:

- What will the salesperson be doing?

- What part of the sales funnel will they own?

- What resources are available to support their primary functions?

- Who will manage them?

- How will you onboard and train them?

- How will they be compensated and is their compensation tied to what they can control or influence?

- What will this person need to guide leads through the sales funnel and how will they track it? Do you have a CRM for them to use?

- How will you evaluate their performance?

If you are yada-yada-yadaing past these questions because you think your process is good enough to hire right now, take a breath. Ask yourself these questions: If any of my salespeople left today, would my business be able to recover? Is the book of business they have attached to my company or the salesperson? If you have the right infrastructure in place, you should be able to maintain your sales and marketing momentum and stability even if someone leaves. Take a careful look at what you have on hand to support your people before you invite someone new to the table.

Do You Need a Salesperson or a Marketer?

Before going any further, ask yourself if what you need for your team is another salesperson or a marketer. A major indicator that you need to carefully consider the answer is how complex your sales process is and at which point in the funnel you need the most help. If you need more leads, you could benefit from a marketer to really double down at your top-of-funnel lead generation. If you have plenty of leads to sift through but need help establishing yourself as a thought leader, you might need a content writer who can create content on your company's behalf demonstrating your thought leadership and expertise. If you've got all the leads you can handle but are having trouble closing them, that's when you are most likely to need a salesperson to come help share the load. Make sure you have clear processes in place and that their job description is accurate.

What Type of Salesperson Is Right for Your Business?

Knowing what your business needs from its people works together with what your people need from the business. As we established in chapter eighteen, everyone has environments where they thrive and individual skill sets to meet particular challenges. This is where your sales assessments come in, where you evaluate people's abilities with account management or business development, whether they need someone else to provide structure and focus or can motivate and manage themselves. By the time you are assessing them, you should know whether you need someone to jump in and hunt for new business or someone responsible for retaining and growing your current customers or if you need a smart, personable salesperson to answer basic questions and facilitate transactions.

Answer the following questions about your sales process to find what you need:

- Do we already have a process in place to generate leads? Do we have enough leads?

- Can we identify businesses in our marketplace that we need someone to go talk to?

- Do we have more of a simple order-taking based business where leads call us with more basic questions (e.g., roofing, landscaping, etc.)?

- Do we have a more complex, solutions-based sale such as technologies or professional services?

- How long is our typical sales cycle, and does it require numerous touchpoints over weeks, months or longer?

- Do we need a salesperson who needs to be highly motivated, self-driven or self-managed, or are we hiring into a very defined role with predictable ways of operating and an established support structure?

These questions should be used during the creation of job descriptions. Without them, there is a risk that the person hiring will give the salesperson too many responsibilities. They should not be expected to invent their own sales processes for the company. If you find yourself in this position, it is important to get clearer and more intentional about what your ideal fit for your company will be.

Don't Forget the Team Manager

You want a sales and marketing team who can operate autonomously, but even the best teams need a coach. Some people appoint leadership specifically to deal with sales and marketing while others choose to bring in a consultant who has a more honed understanding of the sales process. Whoever coaches your sales team should be able to survey the sales funnel or funnels from top to bottom and have all the processes in place to keep your salespeople equipped with the tools they need to succeed. The person needs to possess the following skills and qualities:

- Sales knowledge and skills, with the ability to lead by example and align to your company values and culture (you might consider a player coach as a possible solution)

- Ability to manage up to their boss, down to their direct reports and laterally to leads of other departments

- Ability to advocate for their team to leadership and explaining the current and desired state in a way that people can understand

- Solid grasp of sales and marketing technologies and the ability to either modify it themselves or work with the tech team to map it to the established sales process

- Understanding of KPIs and ability to use qualitative and quantitative data to make decisions on behalf of company and team

It is difficult to find someone who can exhibit all these skills and abilities right away, especially if you already have sales leadership in place. It is possible for someone to learn these skills to fill in the gaps. Reaching out for guidance and, of course, collaboration and alignment with the marketing team helps fulfill the listed needs.

Action Items

- If you don't have a formal sales structure in place, first educate yourself using books, courses, mentorship, etc., to learn about building a sales organization before hiring.

- Build or review job descriptions and ask yourself whether you are asking the salesperson to do or be too many different things. Discern whether the job description applies to one or more than one role.

- Review your sales processes and determine the optimal sales teams to align to that process. Figure out whether you want one or two full stack salespeople or a more team-based approach, where different salespeople handle different stages within the funnel.

- If you currently have a sales manager, evaluate their skills and whether you need to provide them with more resources and training to fill in the gaps.

Conclusion:

Take the Next Step

Here are your key takeaways for sales and marketing alignment.

Congratulations! By making it to the end of this book, you've taken your first step in bringing your sales and marketing teams into alignment for greater efficiency, teamwork and success. We've covered a lot, from why you need a sales and marketing integration strategy in the first place all the way to the nitty-gritty of hiring marketing and sales team members.

We know there is much to learn and many actions to take. Consider this book a reference manual to guide you over time as your company best aligns sales and marketing teams. Return to the book for guidance and words of wisdom, because your sales and alignment journey will be ongoing. You will also gain new insights you may not have caught on your first reading. Revenue growth will follow by implementing our recommendations and by getting buy-in from your teams. We are confident in your success!

Here is a summary of the key topics covered in *Sales & Marketing Alignment*.

Remember to Prioritize Strategy, People and Processes

Sales and marketing teams in the digital age face many challenges and constant, stiff competition. Companies can no longer afford to randomly try sales and marketing tactics and hope they work. Buyers have many options, and a world of information is at their fingertips. They will research a business and product in detail before buying. To survive the competition, you must demonstrate thought leadership and offer excellent content to your buyers. You must connect with buyers through a winning marketing strategy and follow through with consistent sales tactics. There must be synergy between these two strategies. You can no longer afford to wing it and avoid this strategic work.

Precise and consistent sales and marketing processes, including valuable marketing content, requires planning and intentionality followed by expert execution. Talented, skilled and motivated people working together to build those processes and mechanisms are must-have members of your sales and marketing teams. For a reminder about why these three elements are so important, revisit chapters three and six.

Encourage Sales and Marketing Alignment from the Top

Conflict between sales and marketing teams can be minimized with excellent leadership and solid direction from them. Internal biases within the leadership team can result in conflict between the entirety of your sales and marketing teams. The approaches taken by sales and marketing leaders can make or break the success of teams coming into alignment. If they choose not to communicate clearly and coordinate strategies, they are building walls rather than bridges between departments. Leadership can lead by example to shape a culture of respect and cooperation that results in more sales and a stronger ROI. Read more about how leaders can support sales and marketing alignment in chapter five.

Organize People and Tactics with an Integrated Sales and Marketing Funnel

Your ability to create strategies, build processes and align people is directly tied to your understanding of the buyer's journey. Get inside the head of your buyers and learn their pain points and what they desire. This will help you build a road map for how they research, evaluate and buy from your company. The more specific you get in charting the journey of each buyer, the better. Review details about how to do research and planning related to the buyer's journey in chapter seven. Those details matter in understanding the milestones and conversion points people take along the way. Once you know who they are and what their buyer's journey is, you can form your integrated sales and marketing funnel, covered extensively in chapter nine. You can use the funnel to come together and fix problems with lead generation and conversion, as detailed in chapter ten.

This also enables you to assign people on your team to each part of this buyer's journey, from initial research and brand awareness to the completed sales transaction. When the task is approached as a team, mapping an integrated sales and marketing funnel to your buyer's journey ensures your leads don't get stuck in the funnel. Each step between a lead entering the funnel and becoming a customer must be clearly assigned to a team member and must have metrics in place to evaluate sales and marketing progress. Clear milestones and touchpoints along the funnel help chart your progress and provide direction for the marketing team's tactics. We talk more about building these structures in chapter twelve.

Get Clear on Features and Benefits to Best Connect with Buyers

Often sales and marketing teams spend so much time inside their company's processes and systems, they forget to consider what the customer sees from the outside looking in. Being too close to your own company will lead to blind spots.

After building ideal customer personas and mapping the buyer's journey, sales and marketing teams must get aligned on the outcomes buyers expect. Those outcomes are the perceived benefits people want from your solutions. People understand benefits based on the story they use to connect to that product or service. Benefits and story are linked together as the key to writing excellent marketing copy and closing sales. This is a key area for alignment between the teams. Refresh your memory on how to draw these distinctions and create striking messages in chapter eight.

Integrate CRM and Marketing Automation for Aligned Teams

Breaking down sales and marketing silos also requires an in-depth review of technology and the full integration of your CRM with your marketing automation software. Companies failing to do this will be left behind and those that do it well will gain a competitive advantage. Make the most of your CRM and automation tools by keeping these metrics accessible for both the sales and marketing teams. Multiply the impact of these software tools by sharing between the sales and marketing teams the qualitative and quantitative data from marketing automation and the CRM. Chapter thirteen has a wealth of advice for how to use automation by mapping it to your sales funnel.

Value the Work of Your Human Team Members

Don't rely solely on software and technology to drive results. Software is a tool. People will always drive the strategies that get results. Great people and well-used technology form a winning combination for sales and marketing alignment, but this is not the total solution. Your vision for sales and marketing software should be strategic and part of a process to expand your reach, multiply the team's efforts and expand the strengths of your teams. We get into this subject in chapter thirteen and elaborate more on the very human work of leading a team in chapter eighteen.

Get the Right People in the Right Seats

Understanding the way your company sells and getting educated on how to build a sales and marketing organization will give you a rubric for the type of people to get on your team. Before you hire, evaluate what type of sales and marketing skills are needed for your business and what processes will be in place to support the work (and in some cases the learning process) of your people. Use personality assessments to see what their strengths are when it comes to finding new customers and managing existing accounts. From integrated sales and marketing meetings you can learn a lot about your people and how they can bring their talents to their sales funnel responsibilities. Part three, which includes chapters seventeen through twenty, goes into detail about how to hire and lead a successful integrated sales and marketing team.

Embrace Integrated Sales and Marketing Meetings to Support Teamwork

This book has covered much ground on the topic of sales and marketing alignment. It can be overwhelming to many, and you may be wondering where to start. One of the best starting points is an integrated meeting. Bring together members of both the sales and marketing teams and start the process of working together through regular interactions in meetings. This was covered in detail in chapter fourteen.

Meetings are a central tool in breaking down silos. When you have regular, structured sales and marketing meetings, you make space for long-term change and revenue growth. Even if you don't have ways of gathering integrated funnel data, meeting together to co-create sales and marketing processes will give everybody a sense of ownership and an opportunity to unite behind your team's values. If integrating your sales and marketing teams to build the best strategies and processes described in this book seems intimidating, you can't go wrong by starting with regular meetings.

Celebrate Sales and Marketing Wins and Acknowledge the Team

Meetings are a great place to celebrate sales and marketing wins. We guarantee the concepts we have taught in this book will lead to sales and marketing success. When those successes come along, make sure to celebrate these wins with your teams. Taking the time to acknowledge individual and team wins, no matter how small or how big, is one of the best ways to break down the silos between sales and marketing and build trust, a healthy culture and the ability for your organization to effectively work together as a team. Make sure the team shows gratitude to one another in addition to getting recognition from leadership.

You can celebrate more wins than just closed sales. Celebrate meeting your goals at each stage of the sales funnel: booking a certain number of appointments, hitting a target number of webinar attendees or any other way you are successfully moving leads into, down and through the funnel. Sales and marketing teams are very similar to sports teams; they both are successful due to a winning combination of roles and tasks. Make sure you have talented people whose strengths are being used to their fullest potential and who appreciate one another, support their teammates and celebrate wins together.

Develop and Use an Integrated Scorecard

Just like a sports team measures wins and losses and the stats behind those results, so can sales and marketing teams. The scorecard reports on the team's "stats" and measures wins and losses. The scorecard is unique to your organization, and you must take the time to narrow down the most important KPIs to track in this scorecard. It's hard to celebrate sales and marketing wins if you can't see them!

Meetings are a great place to review the integrated scorecard. Make sure it is on the agenda. It will most likely be a key part of the meeting and spark the discussion about what needs to happen to improve results. We give you advice on creating scorecards and coming together as a team to put that data into action in chapters fifteen and sixteen.

Review Action Items and Resources

We've emphasized being mindful of your buyer's journey, but the sales and marketing alignment journey belongs to you and your team! If you want to get moving with concrete action items, we have included some at the end of each chapter. These action items can be used in your integrated meetings for to-do lists and inspirations to best align your company's sales and marketing efforts. It will be hard work, but it will pay off and get you closer to your goals.

For more insights, resources and tools on sales and marketing alignment, please visit Tom's website at intuitivewebsites.com and Karl's website at improvingsalesperformance.com. We wish you the best of luck and success on this path to improving results from your sales and marketing teams.

Glossary

benefits: Positive outcomes from using a product or service that meet customers' needs, provide solutions to their problems and gain what they want.

bottom of the funnel: The point in the integrated sales and marketing funnel at which the buyer's journey ends and the lead makes the decision to buy and become a customer.

buyer's journey: The path that a unique customer persona takes in order to move from their current state through evaluating a company's products or services to deciding about buying.

call to action (CTA): A piece of written content, typically taking the form of an instruction or directive, that asks a user to perform a specific act such as buying, signing up for a mailing list or looking at additional content.

campaign: Coordinated sales and marketing efforts around a central theme or objective and the defined strategies and tactics to bring buyers into and through the sales funnel.

chief executive officer (CEO): The highest-ranking corporate executive in an organization, a CEO is typically responsible for increasing the revenue and value of a business and often serves as its public face.

chief financial officer (CFO): A corporate executive who is responsible for managing the company's finances; their duties often include risk management, planning, and data analysis.

chief information officer (CIO): A corporate executive who manages a company's information technology as well as implementing strategies and processes for processing information within the organization.

chief marketing officer (CMO): A corporate executive responsible for marketing activities within an organization.

chief operating officer (COO): A corporate executive who oversees a company's daily administrative functions and internal operations and is often responsible for overseeing sales processes.

chief technology officer (CTO): A corporate executive who manages technological requirements for the company.

co-creating: Sales and marketing team members coming together to brainstorm and plan solutions in a way that lets everyone provide input and expertise.

content: Online material such as videos, blogs and social media posts providing value to the reader and promoting a company's products or services.

CRM: Standing for "customer relationship management," this technology manages a company's relationships and interactions with customers and potential customers at each stage of the sales cycle; it includes contact management, sales management and salesperson productivity and allows for lead scoring.

features: The functions and characteristics of a product or service.

ideal customer personas: Semifictional representations of a company's ideal customers, which sales and marketing teams build from qualitative and quantitative data.

integrated sales and marketing funnel: A process that leads pass through, from showing an initial interest in marketing materials, to moving through the process of sales and marketing, to eventually buying a product; an organizational structure to categorize leads with similar characteristics into different groups, or stages. The leads at the top of the funnel are the furthest away from a purchase, and those at the bottom of the funnel are ready to buy. (Sometimes referred to as *funnel* or *sales funnel*.)

key performance indicators (KPIs): Data points that are used to evaluate the effectiveness of business development, sales and marketing efforts.

lead magnet: Free item or service that is given away for the purpose of gathering contact details for sales leads; lead magnets can be trial subscriptions, webinars, samples, white papers, e-newsletters or free consultations.

lead scoring: A process of evaluating leads according to where they are in the sales funnel and how close they are to buying, using a numerical system to score or rank a lead based on their actions and estimation of their interest.

marketing and sales design: Defining who a company sells to and the buyer's journey, starting from a lead's awareness of the company to closed business.

marketing automation: A catchall phrase given to software applications that automatically engage with prospects in the funnel, most often via email, based on their online actions (e.g., opening an email or visiting a web page).

marketing qualified lead (MQL): Leads who enter at the top of the integrated sales and marketing funnel, making initial contact via marketing outreach of one type or another. Examples include signing up for a newsletter, downloading a marketing magnet and following a company on social media.

middle of the funnel: A transition point when leads consider moving forward with a solution to their problems; handling leads in this stage takes the coordinated efforts of both sales and marketing teams.

omni-channel digital marketing: A coordinated approach to marketing online that uses consistent messaging and strategy across various channels to interact with customers (e.g., websites, social media, guest blogging).

processes: The steps and systems used to implement sales and marketing strategies, either in individual parts or as a whole.

qualitative data: Feedback and observations gathered from firsthand experience and anecdotal evidence; in a sales and marketing environment, this information is usually gathered by the sales team.

quantitative data: Numerical metrics that indicate how well objectives are being achieved in a sales and marketing organization (e.g., sales numbers, number of leads per stage of the sales and marketing funnel, other KPIs).

return on investment (ROI): A measure of performance that determines the efficiency or profitability of spending on a particular use of funds.

revenue equation: A framework for sales and marketing organizations based on understanding the root causes of sales and marketing problems, then creating systems to solve them. The equation consists of three factors that, when added together, lead to equal revenue stabilization and growth.

sales and marketing placemat: A more advanced version of the sales funnel where each stage of the sales funnel is assigned clear owners with defined responsibilities, associated actions to move the leads from one grouping to the next and KPIs to gain insights to improve the performance of each stage.

sales development representative (SDR): A sales team member who is responsible for reaching out to leads to help determine whether they are qualified.

sales qualified lead (SQL): A lead who is deemed ready for the sales team to get in contact with to close on their level of engagement with sales and marketing materials.

SMBs: An abbreviation for *small- and medium-size businesses*, where a business with 100 or fewer employees is considered small and a business with between 100 and 999 employees is considered medium.

software as a service (SaaS) company: A company that delivers and licenses software that is accessed by users via a subscription model.

strategy: The overarching game plan that sets the direction in which you want to head to reach your sales and marketing objectives.

tactics: The specific steps or actions you take to accomplish an established sales and marketing strategy, which is incorporated into your processes.

teaming: The act coming together with a positive, intentional mindset to reach a shared goal.

top of the funnel: The stage of the sales funnel in which people initially engage with marketing materials and want to learn more; leads at this stage are often called marketing qualified leads (MQLs) and are usually not ready to buy.

Resources

Recommended Reading

Building a StoryBrand: Clarify Your Message So Customers Will Listen by Donald Miller (Harper Collins, 2017)

Contagious: Why Things Catch On by Jonah Berger (Simon & Schuster, 2013)

Don't Make Me Think: A Common Sense Approach to Web Usability (3rd Edition) by Steve Krug (Pearson Education, 2015)

Made to Stick: Why Some Ideas Survive and Others Die by Chip and Dan Heath (Random House, 2007)

Set Up to Win: Three Frameworks to a High Performing Sales Organization by Karl Becker (Improving Sales Performance, 2021)

Winning the Website War: Four Steps to Marketing Success by Thomas Young (Intuitive Websites, 2014)

Recommended Sales and Marketing Tools

We realize there are many options and an ever-expanding set of tools and other resources. We use the following on a routine basis for most B2B engagements.

Analytics
CrazyEgg for heat mapping web pages
Google Analytics and Google Search Console
Google Ads keyword search tool

Assessments
DiSC
Sales Achiever
The Predictive Index

Content Marketing and Social Media
Buffer
Content Marketing Institute
Hootsuite
HubSpot
LinkedIn and Sales Navigator
Pardot
Salesforce
Social Media Examiner
Verblio
Writer's Access

CRM
Leadfeeder.com
HubSpot
Pipedrive
Salesforce-ZoomInfo

Project Management
Asana
Trello

SEO
Search Engine Watch
Neil Patel
SEMRush
ScreamingFrog

The Sales Placemat:

Roles & Responsibilities
Sales Process
KPIs & Performance Management

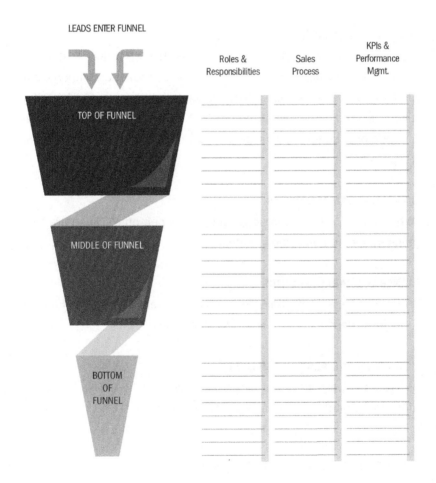

LEADS ENTER FUNNEL

TOP OF FUNNEL

MIDDLE OF FUNNEL

BOTTOM OF FUNNEL

Roles & Responsibilities

Sales Process

KPIs & Performance Mgmt.

Ideal Customer Persona
and the Five-Step Buyer's Journey

Complete this worksheet for each ideal customer persona.

Name

Target Audience Characteristics

Description: Each ideal customer persona has attributes that shape your understanding of the persona. These attributes are important to understand because they provide insights into how to develop effective sales and marketing strategies for that persona. These attributes are personal demographics, general characteristics and job roles and responsibilities.

PERSONAL DEMOGRAPHICS

What are the personal descriptions of the persona? These are their gender, age and possible job titles.

GENERAL CHARACTERISTICS

What are the general characteristics of the persona? Think of this as how you'd describe the persona to a colleague.

JOB ROLES AND RESPONSIBILITIES

What is the persona's job roles and responsibilities? This is how we describe what this persona was hired to do.

The Five-Step Buyer's Journey

Every person goes through a five-step buyer's journey as they navigate their personal or professional life. This journey is associated with the human condition, where we gain self-awareness of our current state, experience and reflect on our challenges and envision a future state where things are improved. Sales design is developed from an understanding of the five steps of the buyer's journey of each persona and applying this knowledge to how sales and marketing communicates with our target audiences. The buyer's journey evolves from an understanding of the current state, to challenges, to desired state, to solutions, to making a purchase decision.

Journey Step One: The Buyer's Current State

Build a snapshot of the persona's work life before they've become aware of their problem or your solutions. Their current state gives a realistic idea of their roles and responsibilities and how those affect them on a personal level. Knowing where they're coming from will help you envision where they are going and how you might help them get there.

- Typical Workday—What is their typical workday like?

    □ How do their daily responsibilities and other's expectations of them impact their personal life?

- Working Environment—What is it like to work at their company or organization?

    □ Describe both positive and negative elements (e.g., how action-packed their day is, external demands made on them, budget-related issues and their level of personal investment in their work).

- Daily Experience—What is most likely happening in their world?

    □ Describe, for example, events they are planning for and external elements that impact the way their job is done.

☐ Describe how these variables affect their job role (i.e., how often they have to multitask, how many projects they manage, what their state of urgency is).

Journey Step Two: The Buyer's Challenges

At this point, the ideal customer persona experiences awareness of the problem or problems they need to solve. Identifying these helps you predict all the circumstances and possibilities that need to be addressed for them to reach an ideal state. It also helps you empathize with what the persona is experiencing. Answer these questions by considering the persona's end goal and job description (e.g., increasing revenue, pleasing stakeholders, putting on an event, purchasing or creating a product that meets their needs and wants).

- Problems—What work problems keep them up at night?

    ☐ Include any challenges they face, both daily and on an ongoing basis.

    ☐ What is their baseline objective that you could provide a solution for?

- Failure—How do they fail at their job?

    ☐ Include any situations that would impact failure or poor performance.

    ☐ Specifically, how would they fail at their baseline objective that you could provide a solution for?

- Stress—What makes their job frustrating or stressful, even when they are not in a state of failure?

□ Include all stress sources (e.g., from fellow employees, vendors, customers, board members and bosses and pressure they may place on themselves).

Journey Step Three The Buyer's Desired State

This is the ultimate ideal scenario that the persona can envision if all their problems were solved. Your persona would naturally want to consider the limitations of budget, time and external expectations. Use the magic wand technique to remove the barrier of reality. It will give you ideas about how your services can exceed their normal needs and expectations.

- Magic Wand Outcomes—If the persona had a fairy godmother who could wave a magic wand and create the future they wanted, what would the outcome look like?

    □ This tool projects a fantastical version of their future state. Make this as perfect as you can, even if it's unrealistic.

    □ What would a dream situation look like for the customer personally? What would it look like for the stakeholders the customer is trying to please?

- Needs—What are the requirements they need to achieve or improve?

    □ Include all the must-have elements of their desired state.

    □ Consider elements that will keep them from their least-desired state: their state of failure.

- Wants—In addition to needs, what else do they want?

    □ Include all the nice-to-have elements of their desired state.

□ List all the bells and whistles they'd like, including for their personal experience, and the most impressive elements of their dream outcome.

Journey Step Four: The Buyer's Solutions

Your persona has more than just the basics to make their future state successful. You need to anticipate the special considerations that are unique to their industry and the people they serve. Also, remember that you are not the only person who can give them a positive outcome; you need to be aware and knowledgeable about everything that they might be considering to solve their problem.

- Options—What options do they have to solve their problems or improve their current state?

  □ Describe as many options as you can (e.g., your company, competitors who do the same thing as you, DIY solutions, switching to a completely different type of solution than what you are offering to meet their goal).

- Considerations—What is the buyer thinking about as they consider the different solutions?

  □ Describe the typical considerations someone in the persona's role would have to consider (e.g., special features and accommodations for them and the stakeholders they serve).

- Evaluation—How does the buyer evaluate and compare all the value these different options can provide for them?

  □ Describe what the buyer would need and how they would evaluate the options.

Journey Step Five: The Buyer's Purchase

Your effort to understand the persona's current state, the problems they're facing, the outcome they want and the alternative solutions available to them, will eventually lead them to the point of purchasing. It's now that you need to be able to address logistical concerns and de-risk their decision to buy from you.

- Buying Process—How does the persona buy a solution?

    - ☐ Consider who is making the ultimate decision. Is it solely up to them? Is there a committee or other internal process?

    - ☐ What financial restrictions do they have, and what aspects of your offering are deal breakers for them (e.g., hard budgetary or payment disbursal restraints, lack of a guarantee, etc.) if they buy through a committee or internal process, including any financial considerations such as terms or financing?

- Confidence and Risk—What does the persona need to increase their confidence in a solution and de-risk their decision?

    - ☐ Describe any actions or resources they would take or want.

    - ☐ Remember who else has a say in this purchase, if applicable, and think about what they will want to see as well.

- Final Step—How does the persona make their final decision to purchase?

    - ☐ Describe the final actions a buyer typically takes to make a purchase for your offering.

Revenue Equation Worksheet

For comprehensive Revenue Equation resources and content, please visit revenueequation.com.

This is an overview of what you will be determining for each factor of your Revenue Equation.

Components of the Revenue Equation Factors		
Foundations + Design + Infrastructure = Revenue Stabilization and Growth		
Foundations	**Design**	**Infrastructure**
Value Proposition Key Differentiators Customer Experience Promise Foundational Messaging	Target Audience Characteristics Ideal Customer Personas The Buyer's Journey Selling Tactics and Assets	Team Roles and Responsibilities Sales Process Sales and Marketing Technology Sales Forecasting and KPIs Performance Management

Sales and Marketing Foundations

On a scale of low to high, how well DEFINED and UNDERSTOOD is each of the following within your organization?	1= Low 10 = High
Problems We Solve: The root problems that your organization solves	1 2 3 4 5 6 7 8 9 10

On a scale of low to high, how well DEFINED and UNDERSTOOD is each of the following within your organization?	1= Low 10 = High
Value Proposition: The way you create value and deliver that value to your clients	1 2 3 4 5 6 7 8 9 10
Key Differentiators: The attributes that clearly separate you from the competition	1 2 3 4 5 6 7 8 9 10
Customer Experience Promise: The defined experiences you want to create for your clients	1 2 3 4 5 6 7 8 9 10
Offerings: The products and/or services your company provides its customers	1 2 3 4 5 6 7 8 9 10
Average Score	

Sales and Marketing Design

On a scale of low to high, how well DEFINED and USED is each of the following within your organization?	1= Low 10 = High
Target Audience Organization: The types of organizations that purchase your offerings	1 2 3 4 5 6 7 8 9 10
Ideal Customer Persona: A hypothetical person suited to purchase your offerings	1 2 3 4 5 6 7 8 9 10
Buyer's Journey: A series of steps buyers go through that represents the purchasing life cycle	1 2 3 4 5 6 7 8 9 10
Campaigns: Defined strategies and tactics to bring buyers into and through the sales funnel	1 2 3 4 5 6 7 8 9 10
Average Score	

Sales and Marketing Infrastructure

On a scale of low to high, how well DEFINED and USED is each of the following within your organization?	1= Low 10 = High
Roles and Responsibilities: Defined ownership of activities within each stage of the sales funnel	1 2 3 4 5 6 7 8 9 10
Sales Process: Structured actions required to cultivate a prospect from lead stage to close	1 2 3 4 5 6 7 8 9 10
Sales and Marketing Technology: Tech used to increase sales funnel efficiency and effectiveness	1 2 3 4 5 6 7 8 9 10
Sales Forecasting and KPIs: Data used to evaluate team and sales funnel performance	1 2 3 4 5 6 7 8 9 10
Performance Management: Process to optimize the sales and marketing team	1 2 3 4 5 6 7 8 9 10
Average Score	

Sales and Marketing Scorecard Example

Here is an example of a high-level scorecard that Karl uses with his clients. This is being represented in a table, but it is typically generated in reports from the client's CRM.

The purpose of the scorecard is to give quick and valuable insights into the overall health and performance of the sales funnel and thus insights into revenue. In this example, there are weekly KPI goal values as well as places to report back the actual values from the prior weeks. Each KPI provides data specific to a particular part of the sales funnel. This enables the sales and marketing team to look at the performance of specific activities as well as the aggregate value of the sales funnel. The scorecard both provides a snapshot of current revenue performance and can be used to forecast future revenue.

Weekly Performance KPIs

KPI	Goal Value	Jan 24– Jan 30	Jan 17– Jan 23	Jan 10– Jan 16	Jan 03– Jan 09	Dec 27– Jan 02
New Social Media Followers	50	55	65	46	54	68
Newsletter Signups	100	101	107	115	98	107
Magnet Downloads	50	45	52	47	51	47
Appointments Generated	20	21	20	23	19	22

KPI	Goal Value	Jan 24– Jan 30	Jan 17– Jan 23	Jan 10– Jan 16	Jan 03– Jan 09	Dec 27– Jan 02
New Sales Revenue	$50,000	$55,000	$46,000	$52,000	$50,000	$49,000
Forecasted Sales (50% Close Rate)	$75,000	$85,000	$78,000	$75,000	$90,000	$88,000
Follow-Up Calls Scheduled	35	38	42	33	33	40
Deal Stage 1 Population	75	80	72	74	72	80
Deal Stage 2 Population	50	52	48	48	46	50
Deal Stage 3 Population	25	22	24	22	27	25

Individual Sales Planner

This Individual Sales Planer is designed to provide a road map for your individual success and integrate into the organization's revenue road map. It is recommended that you update this document each quarter and use it as a communication and accountability tool with your sales manager.

Do the best you can in completing this document. You may not know the answer to each question or know what to put as your answer—that is OK. This is a document to facilitate ideas and architect an intentional path forward to an improved state. The document also serves as a tool to collaborate with your manager, to help the two of you be in conversation and team more effectively.

Table of Contents
- Strengths and Focus Areas
- Motivations and Motivators
- Goals—Personal and Professional
- Daily Prioritization (Activities)
- Community Involvement / Networking / Education
- Sales Targets
- Current Clients—Top Five
- Target List—Top Five
- Success Criteria
- Timeline and Milestones

Strengths and Focus Areas

Insights into your personal strengths and your daily focus areas
What are your strengths?

[strength + description if necessary for clarification]

[strength + description if necessary for clarification]

[strength + description if necessary for clarification]

How could you use more of your strengths each day?
[answer]

What is your focus most days?
[description]

[description]

[description]

What is your ideal focus each day?
[description]

[description]

[description]

What might enable you to spend more time on your ideal focus areas?
[answer]

Motivations and Motivators

Insights into what motivates you personally and professionally
How do you describe motivators?
[answer]

What motivates you personally? Professionally?

Personally
[description]

[description]

[description]

Professionally
　　[description]

　　[description]

　　[description]

How do you feel when you achieve and/or experience your motivations?
　　[answer]

What do you wish you could do more of that would fill you up?
　　[description]

　　[description]

　　[description]

What ideas do you have that would allow you to achieve more of what fills you up?

[answer]

Goals—Personal and Professional

Insights into your personal and professional goals

What are your personal goals for the next ninety days and the next twelve months?

90 Days	12 Months
[description]	[description]
[description]	[description]
[description]	[description]

What are your professional goals for the next ninety days and the next twelve months?

90 Days	12 Months
[description]	[description]
[description]	[description]
[description]	[description]

What are the top three things you want to achieve in the next ninety days and the next twelve months?

90 Days	12 Months
[description]	[description]
[description]	[description]
[description]	[description]

What are the top three things you want to achieve in the next three to five years?

1. [description]

2. [description]

3. [description]

What might get in the way of achieving your goals?
[answer]

Daily Prioritization (Activities)

Insights into your current and optimal daily prioritizations

List out all the activities you spend your time doing most days / most weeks.

This is a brainstorm—just list everything that comes to mind.

[description]

[description]

[description]

[description]

[description]

[description]

What activities (that you just listed) are low value and/or are not relevant to your job?

[answer]

What activities are distractions from your job?

[answer]

Think about all the meetings you are in each week...
How many of these meetings are high value and aligned to your highest and best-use activities (e.g., your job)?

[answer]

How many of these meetings are low value and not aligned to your highest and best-use activities (e.g., your job)?

[answer]

How could you change your week to optimize your job performance?
And better achieve your personal and professional goals?

[answer]

Community Involvement / Networking / Education

Insights into involvement in work-related organizations and learning
List organizations or associations you want to be involved in and your
desired level of involvement.
[name + description of involvement]

[name + description of involvement]

[name + description of involvement]

List networking groups or networking opportunities you want to be
involved in and your desired level of involvement.
[name + description of involvement]

[name + description of involvement]

[name + description of involvement]

List any educational opportunities or skills you want to learn.
[name + description of involvement]

[name + description of involvement]

[name + description of involvement]

How could the organization support you to achieve this involvement?
[answer]

Sales Targets

Insights into your sales targets and how you plan to achieve them
What are your sales targets for the next ninety days?
[values + descriptions]

[values + descriptions]

[values + descriptions]

What is your plan to get there?
   [descriptions]

What are your sales targets for the next twelve months?
   [values + descriptions]

   [values + descriptions]

   [values + descriptions]

What is your plan to get there?
   [descriptions]

What support do you need to help you achieve these sales targets?
   [answer]

Current Clients—Top Five

Strategies and tactics to increase retention and profitability from your top customers or clients

#1 ORGANIZATION NAME: [ENTER HERE]
Contact Name(s):

1. [name]

2. [name]

3. [name]

What do they buy from you?
[describe]

Approximate revenue last year: [value here]
Approximate margin last year: [value here]

What additional challenges, problems or needs do you think they have that you can solve?
[describe]

What additional products or services could you sell them? Use your imagination.

    [describe]

What could you do to increase your margin on their next purchase?

    [describe]

Are you comfortable asking for a referral? If yes, when will you do this? If no, why not?

    [describe]

Go to your contact's LinkedIn profile. List three of their connections you would like to be introduced to:

1. [connection name + company + title]

2. [connection name + company + title]

3. [connection name + company + title]

#2 ORGANIZATION NAME: [ENTER HERE]

Contact Name(s):

1. [name]

2. [name]

3. [name]

What do they buy from you?
[describe]

Approximate revenue last year: [value here]
Approximate margin last year: [value here]

What additional challenges, problems or needs do you think they have that you can solve?
[describe]

What additional products or services could you sell them? Use your imagination.
[describe]

What could you do to increase your margin on their next purchase?
[describe]

Are you comfortable asking for a referral? If yes, when will you do this? If no, why not?
[describe]

Go to your contact's LinkedIn profile. List three of their connections you would like to be introduced to:

1. [connection name + company + title]

2. [connection name + company + title]

3. [connection name + company + title]

#3 ORGANIZATION NAME: [ENTER HERE]

Contact Name(s):

1. [name]

2. [name]

3. [name]

What do they buy from you?
[describe]

Approximate revenue last year: [value here]
Approximate margin last year: [value here]

What additional challenges, problems or needs do you think they have that you can solve?
[describe]

What additional products or services could you sell them? Use your imagination.
[describe]

What could you do to increase your margin on their next purchase?
  [describe]

Are you comfortable asking for a referral? If yes, when will you do this?
If no, why not?
  [describe]

Go to your contact's LinkedIn profile. List three of their connections
you would like to be introduced to:

  1. [connection name + company + title]

  2. [connection name + company + title]

  3. [connection name + company + title]

#4 ORGANIZATION NAME: [ENTER HERE]

Contact Name(s):

1. [name]

2. [name]

3. [name]

What do they buy from you?
[describe]

Approximate revenue last year: [value here]
Approximate margin last year: [value here]

What additional challenges, problems or needs do you think they have
that you can solve?
[describe]

What additional products or services could you sell them? Use your
imagination.
[describe]

What could you do to increase your margin on their next purchase?
[describe]

Are you comfortable asking for a referral? If yes, when will you do this? If no, why not?
[describe]

Go to your contact's LinkedIn profile. List three of their connections you would like to be introduced to:

1. [connection name + company + title]

2. [connection name + company + title]

3. [connection name + company + title]

#5 ORGANIZATION NAME: [ENTER HERE]
Contact Name(s):

1. [name]

2. [name]

3. [name]

What do they buy from you?
   [describe]

Approximate revenue last year: [value here]
Approximate margin last year: [value here]

What additional challenges, problems or needs do you think they have
that you can solve?
   [describe]

What additional products or services could you sell them? Use your
imagination.
   [describe]

What could you do to increase your margin on their next purchase?
[describe]

Are you comfortable asking for a referral? If yes, when will you do this?
If no, why not?
[describe]

Go to your contact's LinkedIn profile. List three of their connections
you would like to be introduced to:

1. [connection name + company + title]

2. [connection name + company + title]

3. [connection name + company + title]

Target List—Top Five

Strategies and tactics to acquire specific customers/clients

#1 ORGANIZATION NAME: [ENTER HERE]
List anyone you know who works there.
   [name + title]

Why is this a good fit for your offerings?
   [describe]

How much revenue could this organization represent for your company?
   [describe]

What ideas do you have to get into this organization?
   [describe]

What is keeping you from going after this target?
   [describe]

#2 ORGANIZATION NAME: [ENTER HERE]

List anyone you know who works there.

    [name + title]

Why is this a good fit for your offerings?

    [describe]

How much revenue could this organization represent for your company?

    [describe]

What ideas do you have to get into this organization?

    [describe]

What is keeping you from going after this target?

    [describe]

#3 ORGANIZATION NAME: [ENTER HERE]

List anyone you know who works there.

[name + title]

Why is this a good fit for your offerings?

[describe]

How much revenue could this organization represent for your company?

[describe]

What ideas do you have to get into this organization?

[describe]

What is keeping you from going after this target?

[describe]

#4 ORGANIZATION NAME: [ENTER HERE]

List anyone you know who works there.

    [name + title]

Why is this a good fit for your offerings?

    [describe]

How much revenue could this organization represent for your company?

    [describe]

What ideas do you have to get into this organization?

    [describe]

What is keeping you from going after this target?

    [describe]

#5 ORGANIZATION NAME: [ENTER HERE]

List anyone you know who works there.

    [name + title]

Why is this a good fit for your offerings?

    [describe]

How much revenue could this organization represent for your company?

    [describe]

What ideas do you have to get into this organization?

    [describe]

What is keeping you from going after this target?

    [describe]

Success Criteria

Metrics to understand and evaluate your success

How will you know that you are achieving personal success?

[answer]

How will you know you are achieving professional success?

[answer]

How will you know that your actions are improving your organization?

[answer]

What are qualitative metrics your plan to use to measure your success?

[answer]

What are quantitative metrics you plan to use to measure your success?

[answer]

Timeline and Milestones

The timelines and key milestones associated with your sales planner

What will you accomplish within the next ninety days?

[answer]

What will you accomplish within the next twelve months?

[answer]

What is the best support for you to achieve these accomplishments?

[answer]

Notes

Acknowledgments

Karl Becker

I would like to start by thanking my wife, Kitty, and my sons, Sam and Morgan, for their love and support as I worked on this book, as well as my parents for teaching me the importance of perseverance in the face of life's challenges. I'm grateful for all the clients and colleagues who have taught me through experience to effectively help teams win and who have provided so many of the lessons shared in this book. Special thanks to Gretchen Lehman and Mike Bobrowski for sharing their thoughts on the content of this book. Finally, I am thankful for my Vistage Trusted Advisor Group for their continued encouragement and to Vistage Chair Don Myers for his perspective and guidance. Also thanks to Emily Einolander for helping see this project through to the end.

Thomas Young

This book would not be possible without the support of several people in my life, beginning with the team of dedicated employees at Intuitive Websites who have helped me better understand what drives client success and how marketing works in the real world. I would also like to thank Don Myers, Lonnie Martin, Drew Day, Kent Wilson, Karen Meehan and the many other Vistage chairs and members I have met during my speaking career with Vistage, who have pushed me to reach higher levels in my business and life. Finally, special thanks to my wife, Lori, for her support through the many ups and downs of running a company and my continued growth as a consultant, speaker and author.

About the Authors

Karl Becker has founded and run numerous companies over the last twenty-five years and now works as a consultant who helps sales organizations reach their revenue goals through a focus on foundations, sales process, teamwork and intentionality. He is the founder of Improving Sales Performance, a consultancy focused on fractional sales and marketing leadership, consulting, coaching, workshops and peer groups. He loves hands-on problem-solving and values the human connections he makes while coaching leadership teams, being part of company transformations and inspiring those he works with to find the best in themselves. He lives in Colorado with his wife and two sons. He is the author of *Set up to Win: Three Frameworks to a High-Performing Sales Organization.* He has a BA in economics from Colorado College and an MBA from the University of Colorado, Boulder. You can learn more about him and his work at improvingsalesperformance.com.

Thomas Young is founder and CEO of Intuitive Websites. He is the author of *Intuitive Selling* and *Winning the Website War: Four Steps to Marketing Success* and has thirty years of experience in marketing and sales, including strategic digital marketing and website marketing. Tom has worked with corporate clients around the country, and his client list is a testament to his ability to work with and get results for organizations.

Tom is an award-winning Vistage speaker who has presented to CEO groups since 2001 and is a recipient of the Vistage Speaker Top Performer Award. He has a BA in communications from the University of Northern Colorado and an MBA from the University of Colorado, Colorado Springs. He enjoys tennis and sports and is an avid musician. Follow Tom on LinkedIn and Twitter.